THE OLYNTHIACS AND THE PHILIPPICS OF DEMOSTHENES

BY DEMOSTHENES TRANSLATED

BY

CHARLES RANN KENNEDY

THE FIRST OLYNTHIAC.

THE ARGUMENT.

Olynthus was a city in Macedonia, at the head of the Toronaic gulf, and north of the peninsula of Pallene. It was colonized by a people from Chalcis in Euboea, and commanded a large district called Chalcidice, in which there were thirty-two cities. Over all this tract the sway of Olynthus was considerable, and she had waged wars anciently with Athens and Sparta, and been formidable to Philip's predecessors on the throne of Macedon. Soon after Philip's accession, the Olynthians had disputes with him, which were at first accommodated, and he gratified them by the cession of Anthemus. They then joined him in a war against Athens, and he gave up to them Potidaea, which had yielded to their united arms. After the lapse of some years, during which Philip had greatly increased his power, and acquired considerable influence in Thessaly and Thrace, the Olynthians became alarmed, and began to think him too dangerous a neighbor. The immediate cause of rupture was an attack which he made on one of the Chalcidian towns. An embassy was instantly sent to Athens, to negotiate an alliance. Philip, considering this as an infraction of their treaty with him, declared war against them, and invaded their territory. A second embassy was sent to Athens, pressing for assistance. The question was debated in the popular assembly. Demades, an orator of considerable ability, but profligate character, opposed the alliance. Many speakers were heard; and at length Demosthenes rose to support the prayer of the embassy, delivering one of those clear and forcible speeches, which seldom failed to make a strong impression on his audience. The alliance was accepted, and succors voted.

The orator here delicately touches on the law of Eubulus, which had made it capital to propose that the Theoric fund should be applied to military service. This fund was in fact the surplus revenue of the civil administration, which by the ancient law was appropriated to the defense of the commonwealth; but it had by various means been diverted from that purpose, and expended in largesses to the people, to enable them to attend the theatre, and other public shows and amusements. The law of Eubulus perpetuated this abuse. (See my article Theorica in the Archaeological Dictionary.) Demosthenes, seeing the necessity of a war supply, hints that this absurd law ought to be abolished, but does not openly propose it.

There has been much difference of opinion among the learned as to the order of the three Olynthiac orations; nor is it certain, whether they were spoken on the occasion of one embassy, or several embassies. The curious may consult Bishop Thirlwall's Appendix to the fifth volume of his Grecian History, and Jacobs' Introduction to his translation. I have followed the common order, as adopted by Bekker, whose edition of Demosthenes is the text of this translation; and indeed my opinion is, on the whole, in favor of preserving the common order, though the plan of this work prevents my entering into controversy on the question. To enable the reader more fully to understand the following orations, I have in an Appendix to this volume given a brief account of Olynthus, showing its position with reference to Macedonia, and the importance of its acquisition to Philip. The historical abstract prefixed to this volume is intended chiefly to assist the reader in reference to dates. Such occurrences only are noticed as may be useful to illustrate Demosthenes.

I believe, men of Athens, you would give much to know, what is the true policy to be adopted in the present matter of inquiry. This being the case, you should be willing to hear with attention those who offer you their counsel. Besides that you will have the benefit of all preconsidered advice, I esteem it part of your good fortune, that many fit suggestions will occur to some speakers at the moment, so that from them all you may easily choose what is profitable.

The present juncture, Athenians, all but proclaims aloud, that you must yourselves take these affairs in hand, if you care for their success. I know not how we seem disposed in the matter. [Footnote: This is a cautious way of hinting at the general reluctance to adopt a vigorous policy. And the reader will observe the use of the first person, whereby the orator includes himself in the same insinuation.] My own opinion is, vote succor immediately, and make the speediest preparations for sending it off from Athens, that you may not incur the same mishap as before; send also embassadors, to announce this, and watch the proceedings. For the danger is, that this man, being unscrupulous and clever at turning events to account, making concessions when it suits him, threatening at other times, (his threats may well be believed,) slandering us and urging our absence against us, may convert and wrest to his use some of our main resources. Though, strange to say, Athenians, the very cause of Philip's strength is a circumstance favorable to you. [Footnote: After alarming the people by showing the strength of their adversary, he turns off skillfully to a topic of encouragement.] His having it in his sole power to publish or conceal his designs, his being at the same time general, sovereign, paymaster, and every where accompanying his army, is a great advantage for quick and timely operations in war; but, for a peace with the Olynthians, which he would gladly make, it has a contrary effect. For it is plain to the Olynthians, that now they are fighting, not for glory or a slice of territory, but to save their country from destruction and servitude. They know how he treated those Amphipolitans who surrendered to him their city, and those Pydneans who gave him admittance. [Footnote: Amphipolis was a city at the head of the Strymonic gulf, in that part of Macedonia which approaches western Thrace. It had been built formerly by an Athenian colony, and was taken by the Spartan general Brasidas in the Peloponnesian war. Ever since Athens regained her character of an imperial state, she had desired to recover Amphipolis, which was important for its maritime position, its exportation of iron, and especially from the vicinity of the forests near the Strymon, which afforded an inexhaustible supply of ship-timber. But she had never been able to accomplish that object. Philip, who at that time possessed no maritime town of importance, was for obvious reasons anxious to win Amphipolis for himself; and he got possession of it partly by force of arms, partly by the treachery of certain Amphipolitans who were attached to his interest. It seems the Athenians had been amused by a promise of Philip to give up the town to them. The non-performance of this compact led to their first long war with him. Immediately after the capture of Amphipolis, Philip marched against Pydna, and was admitted into the town.] And generally, I believe, a despotic power is mistrusted by free states, especially if their dominions are adjoining. All this being known to you, Athenians, all else of importance considered, I say, you must take heart and spirit, and apply yourselves more than ever to the war, contributing promptly, serving personally, leaving nothing undone. No plea or pretense is left you for declining your duty. What you were all so clamorous about, that the Olynthians should be pressed into a war with Philip, has of itself come to pass, [Footnote: Compare Virgil, Aen. ix. 6.

Turne, quod optanti Divum promittere nemo

Auderet, volvenda dies en attulit ultro.]

and in a way most advantageous to you. For, had they undertaken the war at your instance, they might have been slippery allies, with minds but half resolved perhaps: but since they hate him on a quarrel of their own, their enmity is like to endure on account of their fears and their wrongs. You must not then, Athenians, forego this lucky opportunity, nor commit the error which you have often done heretofore. For example, when we returned from succoring the Euboeans, and Hierax and Stratocles of Amphipolis came to this platform, [Footnote: The hustings from which the speakers addressed the people. It was cut to the height of ten feet out of the rock which formed the boundary wall of the assembly; and was ascended by a flight of steps.] urging us to sail and receive possession of their city, if we had shown the same zeal for ourselves as for the safety of Euboea, you would have held Amphipolis then and been rid of all the troubles that ensued. Again, when news came that Pydna, [Footnote: Potidaea was in the peninsula of Pallene, near Olynthus, and was therefore given by Philip to the Olynthians, as mentioned in the argument. Methone and Pydna are on the Macedonian coast approaching Thessaly. Pagasae is a Thessalian town in the Magnesian district. It was the sea-port of Pherae, capital of the tyrant Lycophron, against whom Philip was invited to assist the Thessalians. Philip overcame Lycophron, and restored republican government at Pherae; but Pagasae he garrisoned himself, and also Magnesia, a coast-town in the same district.] Potidaea, Methone, Pagasae, and the other places (not to waste time in enumerating them) were besieged, had we to any one of these in the first instance carried prompt and reasonable succor, we should have found Philip far more tractable and humble now. But, by always neglecting the present, and imagining the future would shift for itself, we, O men of Athens, have exalted Philip, and made him greater than any king of Macedon ever was. Here then is come a crisis, this of Olynthus, self-offered to the state, inferior to none of the former. And methinks, men of Athens, any man fairly estimating what the gods have done for us, notwithstanding many untoward circumstances, might with reason be grateful to them. Our numerous losses in war may justly be charged to our own negligence; but that they happened not long ago, and that an alliance, to counterbalance them, is open to our acceptance, I must regard as manifestations of divine favor. It is much the same as in money matters. If a man keep what he gets, he is thankful to fortune; if he lose it by imprudence, he loses withal his memory of the obligation. So in political affairs, they who misuse their opportunities forget even the good which the gods send them; for every prior event is judged commonly by the last result. Wherefore, Athenians, we must be exceedingly careful of our future measures, that by amendment therein we may efface the shame of the past. Should we abandon these men [Footnote: Here he points to the Olynthian embassadors.] too, and Philip reduce Olynthus, let any one tell me, what is to prevent him marching where he pleases? Does any one of you, Athenians, compute or consider the means, by which Philip, originally weak, has become great? Having first taken Amphipolis, then Pydna, Potidaea next, Methone afterward, he invaded Thessaly. Having ordered matters at Pherae, Pagasae, Magnesia, every where exactly as he pleased, he departed for Thrace; where, after displacing some kings and establishing others, he fell sick; again recovering, he lapsed not into indolence, but instantly attacked the Olynthians. I omit his expeditions to Illyria and Paeonia, that against Arymbas, [Footnote: Arymbas was a king of the Molossians in Epirus, and uncle of Olympias, Philip's wife.] and some others.

Why, it may be said, do you mention all this now? That you, Athenians, may feel and understand both the folly of continually abandoning one thing after another, and the activity which forms part of Philip's habit and existence, which makes it impossible for him to rest content with his achievements. If it be his principle, ever to do more than he has done, and yours, to apply yourselves vigorously to nothing, see what the end promises to be. Heavens! which of you is so simple as not to know, that the war yonder will soon be here, if we are careless? And should this happen, I fear, O Athenians, that as men who thoughtlessly borrow on large interest, after a brief accommodation, lose their estate, so will it be with us; found to have paid dear for our idleness and self-indulgence, we shall be reduced to many hard and unpleasant shifts, and struggle for the salvation of our country.

To censure, I may be told, is easy for any man; to show what measures the case requires, is the part of a counselor. I am not ignorant, Athenians, that frequently, when any disappointment happens, you are angry, not with the parties in fault, but with the last speakers on the subject; yet never, with a view to self-protection, would I suppress what I deem for your interest. I say then, you must give a two-fold assistance here; first, save the Olynthians their towns, [Footnote: The Chalcidian towns. See the Argument. Philip commenced his aggressions upon the Olynthians by reducing several of these.] and send out troops for that purpose; secondly, annoy the enemy's country with ships and other troops; omit either of these courses, and I doubt the expedition will be fruitless. For should he, suffering your incursion, reduce Olynthus, he will easily march to the defense of his kingdom; or, should you only throw succor into Olynthus, and he, seeing things out of danger at home, keep up a close and vigilant blockade, he must in time prevail over the besieged. Your assistance therefore must be effective, and two-fold.

Such are the operations I advise. As to a supply of money: you have money, Athenians; you have a larger military fund than any people; and you receive it just as you please. If ye will assign this to your troops, ye need no further supply; otherwise ye need a further, or rather ye have none at all. How then? some man may exclaim: do you move that this be a military fund? Verily, not I. [Footnote: There is some studied obscurity in this passage, owing to the necessity under which the speaker lay of avoiding the penalty of the law and a little quiet satire on his countrymen, who seemed desirous of eating their pudding and having it too. The logic of the argument runs thus—My opinion is, that we ought to have a military fund, and that no man should receive public money, without performing public service. However, as you prefer taking the public money to pay for your places at the festivals, I will not break the law by moving to apply that money to another purpose. Only you gain nothing by it; for, as the troops must be paid, there must be an extraordinary contribution, or property tax, to meet the exigency of the case.] My opinion indeed is, that there should be soldiers raised, and a military fund, and one and the same regulation for receiving and performing what is due; only you just without trouble take your allowance for the festivals. It remains then, I imagine, that all must contribute, if much be wanted, much, if little, little. Money must be had; without it nothing proper can be done. Other persons propose other ways and means. Choose which ye think expedient; and put hands to the work, while it is yet time.

It may be well to consider and calculate how Philip's affairs now stand. They are not, as they appear, or as an inattentive observer might pronounce, in very good trim, or in the most favorable position. He would never have commenced this war, had he imagined he must fight. He expected to carry every thing on the first advance, and has been mistaken. This disappointment is one thing that troubles and dispirits him; another is, the state of Thessaly. [Footnote: Philip's influence in Thessaly was of material assistance to him in his ambitious projects. It was acquired in this way. The power established by Jason of Pherae, who raised himself to a sort of royal authority under the title of Tagus, had devolved upon Lycophron. His sway extended more or less over the whole of Thessaly; but was, if not generally unpopular, at least unacceptable to the great families in the northern towns, among whom the Aleuadae of Larissa held a prominent place. They invoked Philip's aid, while Lycophron was assisted by the Phocian Onomarchus. After various success, Onomarchus was defeated and slain, and Lycophron expelled from Pherae. This established Philip's influence, and led to his being afterward called in to terminate the Sacred war. How far the assertions of Demosthenes, respecting the discontent of the Thessalians, are true, can not exactly be told. They are confirmed, however, in some degree by the fact, that at the close of the Sacred war Philip restored to them Magnesia. A new attempt by the regnant family caused Philip again to be invited, and Thessaly became virtually a province of Macedonia. Among other advantages therefrom was the aid of a numerous cavalry, for which Thessaly was famous.] That people were always, you know, treacherous to all men; and just as they ever have been, they are to Philip. They have resolved to demand the restitution of Pagasae, and have prevented his fortifying Magnesia; and I was told, they would no longer allow him to take the revenue of their harbors and markets, which they say should be applied to the public business of Thessaly, not received by Philip. Now, if he be deprived of this fund, his means will be much straitened for paying his mercenaries. And surely we must suppose, that Paeonians and Illyrians, and all such people, would rather be free and independent than under subjection; for they are unused to obedience, and the man is a tyrant. So report says, and I can well believe it; for undeserved success leads weak-minded men into folly; and thus it appears often, that to maintain prosperity is harder than to acquire it. Therefore must you, Athenians, looking on his difficulty as your opportunity, assist cheerfully in the war, sending embassies where required, taking arms yourselves, exciting all other people; for if Philip got such an opportunity against us, and there was a war on our frontier, how eagerly think ye he would attack you! Then are you not ashamed, that the very damage which you would suffer, if he had the power, you dare not seize the moment to inflict on him?

And let not this escape you, Athenians, that you have now the choice, whether you shall fight there, or he in your country. If Olynthus hold out, you will fight there and distress his dominions, enjoying your own home in peace. If Philip take that city, who shall then prevent his marching here? Thebans? I wish it be not too harsh to say, they will be ready to join in the invasion. Phocians? who can not defend their own country without your assistance. Or some other ally? But, good sir, he will not desire! Strange indeed, if, what he is thought fool-hardy for prating now, this he would not accomplish if he might. As to the vast difference between a war here or there, I fancy there needs no argument. If you were obliged to be out yourselves for thirty days only, and take the necessaries for camp-service from the land, (I mean, without an enemy therein,) your agricultural population would sustain, I believe, greater damage than what the whole expense of the late war [Footnote: The Amphipolitan war, said to have cost fifteen hundred talents.] amounted to. But if a war should come, what damage must be expected? There is the insult too, and the disgrace of the thing, worse than any damage to right-thinking men.

On all these accounts, then, we must unite to lend our succor, and drive off the war yonder; the rich, that, spending a little for the abundance which they happily possess, they may enjoy the residue in security; the young, [Footnote: Strictly, those of the military age, which was from eighteen years to sixty. Youths between eighteen and twenty were liable only to serve in Attica, and were chiefly employed to garrison the walls. Afterward they were compellable to perform any military service, under the penalty of losing their privileges as citizens. The expression in the text, it will be seen, is not rendered with full accuracy; as those of the military age can only be called young by comparison. But a short and apt antithesis was needed. Sometimes I have "the service-able" or "the able-bodied." Jacobs: die waffenfahigen Junglinge, and elsewhere, die Rustige.] that, gaining military experience in Philip's territory, they may become redoubtable champions to preserve their own; the orators, that they may pass a good account [Footnote: Every man, who is required to justify the acts for which he is responsible, may be said to be "called to account." But Demosthenes spoke with peculiar reference to those accounts, which men in official situations at Athens were required to render at the close of their administration.] of their statesmanship; for on the result of measures will depend your judgment of their conduct. May it for every cause be prosperous.

THE SECOND OLYNTHIAC.

THE ARGUMENT.

The Athenians had voted an alliance with the Olynthians, and resolved to send succors. But the sending of them was delayed, partly by the contrivance of the opposite faction, partly from the reluctance of the people themselves to engage in a war with Philip. Demosthenes stimulates them to exertion, and encourages them, by showing that Philip's power is not so great as it appears.

On many occasions, men of Athens, one may see the kindness of the gods to this country manifested, but most signally, I think, on the present. That here are men prepared for a war with Philip, possessed of a neighboring territory and some power, and (what is most important) so fixed in their hostility, as to regard any accommodation with him as insecure, and even ruinous to their country; this really appears like an extraordinary act of divine beneficence. It must then be our care, Athenians, that we are not more unkind to ourselves than circumstances have been; as it would be a foul, a most foul reproach, to have abandoned not only cities and places that once belonged to us, but also the allies and advantages provided by fortune.

To dilate, Athenians, on Philip's power, and by such discourse to incite you to your duty, I think improper: and why? Because all that may be said on that score involves matter of glory for him, and misconduct on our part. The more he has transcended his repute, [Footnote: Jacobs otherwise: uber sein Verdienst gelungen.] the more is he universally admired; you, as you have used your advantages unworthily, have incurred the greater disgrace. This topic, then, I shall pass over. Indeed, Athenians, a correct observer will find the source of his greatness here, [Footnote: In this assembly, by the contrivance of venal orators, or through the supineness of the people. In the first Philippic there is a more pointed allusion to the practices of Philip's adherents, who are charged with sending him secret intelligence of what passed at home. Such men as Aristodemus, Neoptolemus, perhaps Demades and others are referred to. Aeschines had not yet begun to be a friend of Philip.] and not in himself. But of measures, for which Philip's partisans deserve his gratitude and your vengeance, I see no occasion to speak now. Other things are open to me, which it concerns you all to know, and which must, on a due examination, Athenians, reflect great disgrace on Philip. To these will I address myself.

To call him perjured and treacherous, without showing what he has done, might justly be termed idle abuse. But to go through all his actions and convict him in detail, will take, as it happens, but a short time, and is expedient, I think, for two reasons: first, that his baseness may appear in its true light; secondly, that they, whose terror imagines Philip to be invincible, may see he has run through all the artifices by which he rose to greatness, and his career is just come to an end. I myself, men of Athens, should most assuredly have regarded Philip as an object of fear and admiration, had I seen him exalted by honorable conduct; but observing and considering I find, that in the beginning, when certain persons drove away the Olynthians who desired a conference with us, he gained over our simplicity by engaging to surrender Amphipolis, and to execute the secret article [Footnote: A secret intrigue was carried on between Philip and the Athenians, by which he engaged to put Amphipolis in their hands, but on the understanding that they would deliver up Pydna to him. Demosthenes only mentions the former part of the arrangement, the latter not being honorable to his countrymen.] once so famous; afterward he got the friendship of the Olynthians, by taking Potidaea from you, wronging you his former allies, and delivering it to them; and lastly now the Thessalians, by promising to surrender Magnesia, and undertake the Phocian war on their behalf. In short, none who have dealt with him has he not deceived. He has risen by conciliating and cajoling the weakness of every people in turn who knew him not. As, therefore, by such means he rose, when every people imagined he would advance their interest, so ought he by the same means to be pulled down again, when the selfish aim of his whole policy is exposed. To this crisis, O Athenians, are Philip's affairs come; or let any man stand forward and prove to me, or rather to you, that my assertions, are false, or that men whom Philip has once overreached will trust him hereafter, or that the Thessalians who have been degraded into servitude would not gladly become free.

But if any among you, though agreeing in these statements, thinks that Philip will maintain his power by having occupied forts and havens and the like, this is a mistake. True, when a confederacy subsists by good-will, and all parties to the war have a common interest, men are willing to co-operate and bear hardships and persevere. But when one has grown strong, like Philip, by rapacity and artifice, on the first pretext, the slightest reverse, all is overturned and broken up. [Footnote: The original [Greek: anechaitise] is "shakes off," or "throws off," as a horse does his rider, when he rears and tosses up his neck. It will be observed that Demosthenes is very high-flown in his language here, passing from one metaphor to another. Leland translates these words, "overthrows him, and all his greatness is dashed at once to the ground." Francis: "hath already shaken off the yoke and dissolved their alliance." Wilson: "turneth all things upside down and layeth it flat in the end." Auger, better: suffisent pour l' ebranler et la dissoudre. Jacobs: reicht Alles umzusturzen, und aufzulosen. Pabst, very nearly the same.] Impossible is it,— impossible, Athenians,—to acquire a solid power by injustice and perjury and falsehood. Such things last for once, or for a short period; maybe, they blossom fairly with hope; [Footnote: So in Henry VIII. Act iii. Sc. 2.

> Such is the state of man: to-day he puts forth
> The tender leaves of hope, to-morrow blossoms,
> And wears his blushing honors thick upon him.]

but in time they are discovered and drop away. [Footnote: Like the leaves of a flower; pursuing the last metaphor. So says Moore, in The Last Rose of Summer: "the gems drop away." Jacobs: fallt sie von selbst zusammen. Pabst: sturet in sich selbst zusammen.] As a house, a ship, or the like, ought to have the lower parts firmest, so in human conduct, I ween, the principle and foundation should be just and true. But this is not so in Philip's conduct.

I say, then, we should at once aid the Olynthians, (the best and quickest way that can be suggested will please me most,) and send an embassy to the Thessalians, to inform some of our measures, and to stir up the rest; for they have now resolved to demand Pagasae, and remonstrate about Magnesia. But look to this, Athenians, that our envoys shall not only make speeches, but have some real proof that we have gone forth as becomes our country, and are engaged in action. All speech without action appears vain and idle, but especially that of our commonwealth; as the more we are thought to excel therein, the more is our speaking distrusted by all. You must show yourselves greatly reformed, greatly changed, contributing, serving personally, acting promptly, before any one will pay attention to you. And if ye will perform these duties properly and becomingly, Athenians, not only will it appear that Philip's alliances are weak and precarious, but the poor state of his native empire and power will be revealed.

To speak roundly, the Macedonian power and empire is very well as a help, as it was for you in Timotheus' time against the Olynthians; likewise for them against Potidaea the conjunction was important; and lately it aided the Thessalians in their broils and troubles against the regnant house: and the accession of any power, however small, is undoubtedly useful. But the Macedonian is feeble of itself, and full of defects. The very operations which seem to constitute Philip's greatness, his wars and his expeditions, have made it more insecure than it was originally. Think not, Athenians, that Philip and his subjects have the same likings. He desires glory, makes that his passion, is ready for any consequence of adventure and peril, preferring to a life of safety the honor of achieving what no Macedonian king ever did before. They have no share in the glorious result; ever harassed by these excursions up and down, they suffer and toil incessantly, allowed no leisure for their employments or private concerns, unable even to dispose of their hard earnings, the markets of the country being closed on account of the war. By this then may easily be seen, how the Macedonians in general are disposed to Philip. His mercenaries and guards, indeed, have the reputation of admirable and well-trained soldiers, but, as I heard from one who had been in the country, a man incapable of falsehood, they are no better than others. For if there be any among them experienced in battles and campaigns, Philip is jealous of such men and drives them away, he says, wishing to keep the glory of all actions to himself; his jealousy (among other failings) being excessive. Or if any man be generally good and virtuous, unable to bear Philip's daily intemperances, drunkenness, and indecencies, [Footnote: The original signifies a certain lascivious dance, which formed a part of riotous festivities. We gather from history that the orator's description here is not wholly untrue, though exaggerated. Thirlwall thus writes of Philip: "There seem to have been two features in his character which, in another station, or under different circumstances, might have gone near to lower him to an ordinary person, but which were so controlled by his fortune as to contribute not a little to his success. He appears to have been by his temperament prone to almost every kind of sensual pleasure; but as his life was too busy to allow him often to indulge his bias, his occasional excesses wore the air of an amiable condescension. So his natural humor would perhaps have led him too often to forget his dignity in his intercourse with his inferiors; but to Philip, the great king, the conqueror, the restless politician, these intervals of relaxation occurred so rarely, that they might strengthen his influence with the vulgar, and could never expose him to contempt." It has been observed, that Philips partiality for drinking and dancing, his drollery, and a dash of scurrility in his character, endeared him especially to the Thessalians. See Jacobs' note on this passage.] he is pushed aside and accounted as nobody. The rest about him are brigands and parasites, and men of that character, who will get drunk and perform dances which I scruple to name before you. My information is undoubtedly true; for persons whom all scouted here as worse rascals than mountebanks, Callias the town-slave and the like of him, antic-jesters, [Footnote: [Greek: Mimous geloion], players of drolls, mimes, or farces. Our ancient word droll signifies, like [Greek: mimos], both the actor and the thing acted.] and composers of ribald songs to lampoon their companions, such persons Philip caresses and keeps about him. Small matters these may be thought, Athenians, but to the wise they are strong indications of his character and wrong-headedness. Success perhaps throws a shade over them now; prosperity is a famous hider of such blemishes; but, on any miscarriage, they will be fully exposed. And this (trust me, Athenians) will appear in no long time, if the gods so will and you determine. For as in the human body, a man in health feels not partial ailments, but, when illness occurs, all are in motion, whether it be a rupture or a sprain or any thing else unsound; so with states and monarchs, while they wage eternal war, their weaknesses are undiscerned by most men, but the tug of a frontier war betrays all.

If any of you think Philip a formidable opponent, because they see he is fortunate, such reasoning is prudent, Athenians. Fortune has indeed a great preponderance—nay, is every thing, in human affairs. Not but that, if I had the choice, I should prefer our fortune to Philip's, would you but moderately perform your duty. For I see you have many more claims to the divine favor than he has. But we sit doing nothing; and a man idle himself can not require even his friends to act for him, much less the gods. No wonder then that he, marching and toiling in person, present on all occasions, neglecting no time or season, prevails over us delaying and voting and inquiring. I marvel not at that; the contrary would have been marvelous, if we doing none of the duties of war had beaten one doing all. But this surprises me, that formerly, Athenians, you resisted the Lacedaemonians for the rights of Greece, and rejecting many opportunities of selfish gain, to secure the rights of others, expended your property in contributions, and bore the brunt of the battle; yet now you are both to serve, slow to contribute, in defense of your own possessions, and, though you have often saved the other nations of Greece collectively and individually, under your own losses you sit still. This surprises me, and one thing more, Athenians; that not one of you can reckon, how long your war with Philip has lasted, and what you have been doing while the time has passed. You surely know, that while you have been delaying, expecting others to act, accusing, trying one another, expecting again, doing much the same as ye do now, all the time has passed away. Then are ye so senseless, Athenians, as to imagine, that the same measures, which have brought the country from a prosperous to a poor condition, will bring it from a poor to a prosperous? Unreasonable were this and unnatural; for all things are easier kept than gotten. The war now has left us nothing to keep; we have all to get, and the work must be done by ourselves. I say then, you must contribute money, serve in person with alacrity, accuse no one, till you have gained your objects; then, judging from facts, honor the deserving, punish offenders; let there be no pretenses or defaults on your own part for you can not harshly scrutinize the conduct of others, unless you have done what is right yourselves. Why, think you, do all the generals [Footnote: A system of employing mercenary troops sprang up at the close of the Peloponnesian war, when there were numerous Grecian bands accustomed to warfare and seeking employment. Such troops were eagerly sought for by the Persian satraps and their king, by such men as Jason of Pherae, Dionysius of Syracuse, or Philomelus of Phocis. Athens, which had partially employed mercenaries before, began to make use of them on a large scale, while her citizens preferred staying at home, to attend to commerce, politics, and idle amusements. The ill effects however were soon apparent. Athenian generals, ill supplied with money, and having little control over their followers, were tempted or obliged to engage in enterprises unconnected with, and often adverse to, the interests of their country. Sometimes the general, as well as the troops, was an alien, and could be very little depended on. Such a person was Charidemus, a native of Oreus in Euboea, who commenced his career as captain of a pirate vessel. He was often in the service of Athens, but did her more harm than good. See my article Mercenarii, Arch. Dict.] whom you commission avoid this war, and seek wars of their own? (for of the generals too must a little truth be told.) Because here the prizes of the war are yours; for example, if Amphipolis be taken, you will immediately recover it; the commanders have all the risk and no reward. But in the other case the risks are less, and the gains belong to the commanders and soldiers; Lampsacus, [Footnote: Chares, the Athenian general, was said to have received these Asiatic cities from Artabazus, the Persian satrap, in return for the service he had performed. Probably it was some authority or privileges in those cities, not the actual dominion, that was conferred upon him. Sigeum, which is near the mouth of the Hellespont, and was a convenient situation for his adventures, was the ordinary residence of Chares.] Sigeum, the vessels which they plunder. So they proceed to secure their several interests: you, when you look at the bad state of your affairs, bring the generals to trial; but when they get a hearing and plead these necessities, you dismiss them. The result is that, while you are quarreling and divided, some holding one opinion, some another, the commonwealth goes wrong. Formerly, Athenians, you had boards [Footnote: This refers to the institution of the [Greek: summoriai], or boards for management of the property-tax at Athens, as to which see Appendix IV. The argument of Demosthenes is as follows—The three hundred wealthier citizens, who were associated by law for purposes of taxation, had become a clique for political purposes, with an orator at their head, (he intentionally uses the term [Greek: haegemon], chairman of the board,) to conduct the business of the assembly, while they stood to shout and applaud his speeches. The general, who held a judicial court to decide disputes about the property-tax, and who in matters of state ought to be independent, was subservient to the orator, who defended him in the popular assembly.] for taxes; now you have boards for politics. There is an orator presiding on either side, a general under him, and three hundred men to shout; the rest of you are attached to the one party or the other. This you must leave off; be yourselves again; establish a general liberty of speech, deliberation, and action. If some are appointed to command as with royal authority, some to be ship-captains, tax-payers, soldiers by compulsion, others only to vote against them, and help in nothing besides, no duty will be seasonably performed; the aggrieved parties will still fail you, and you will have to punish them instead of your enemies. I say, in short; you must all fairly contribute, according to each man's ability; take your turns of service till you have all been afield; give every speaker a hearing, and adopt the best counsel, not what this or that person advises. If ye act thus, not only will ye praise the speaker at the moment, but yourselves afterward, when the condition of the country is improved.

THE THIRD OLYNTHIAC.

THE ARGUMENT.

The Athenians had dispatched succors to Olynthus, and received, as Libanius says, some favorable intelligence; more probably, however, some vague rumors, which led them to imagine the danger was for the time averted. They began, very prematurely, as the result showed, to be confident of success, and talked of punishing Philip for his presumption. In this they were encouraged by certain foolish orators, who sought to flatter the national prejudices. Demosthenes in this oration strives to check the arrogance of the people; reminds them of the necessity of defensive rather than offensive measures, and especially of the importance of preserving their allies. He again adverts (and this time more boldly) to the law of Eubulus, which he intimates ought to be repealed; and he exhorts the Athenians generally to make strenuous exertions against Philip,

Not the same ideas, men of Athens, are presented to me, when I look at our condition and when at the speeches which are delivered. The speeches, I find, are about punishing Philip; but our condition is come to this, that we must mind we are not first damaged ourselves. Therefore, it seems to me, these orators commit the simple error of not laying before you the true subject of debate. That once we might safely have held our own and punished Philip too, I know well enough; both have been possible in my own time, not very long ago. But now, I am persuaded, it is sufficient in the first instance to effect the preservation of our allies. When this has been secured, one may look out for revenge on Philip; but before we lay the foundation right, I deem it idle to talk about the end.

The present crisis, O Athenians, requires, if any ever did, much thought and counsel. Not that I am puzzled, what advice to give in the matter; I am only doubtful, in what way, Athenians, to address you thereupon. For I have been taught both by hearsay and experience, that most of your advantages have escaped you, from unwillingness to do your duty, not from ignorance. I request you, if I speak my mind, to be patient, and consider only, whether I speak the truth, and with a view to future amendment. You see to what wretched plight we are reduced by some men haranguing for popularity.

I think it necessary, however, first to recall to your memory a few past events. You remember, Athenians, when news came three or four years ago, that Philip was in Thrace beieging Heraeum. [Footnote: A fortress on the Propontis,(now Sea of Marmora,) near Perinthus. This was a post of importance to the Athenians, who received large supplies of corn from that district.] It was then the fifth month, [Footnote: Corresponding nearly to our November. The Attic year began in July, and contained twelve lunar months, of alternately 29 and 30 days. The Greeks attempted to make the lunar and solar courses coincide by cycles of years, but fell into great confusion. See Calendarium in Arch. Dict.] and after much discussion and tumult in the assembly you resolved to launch forty galleys, that every citizen under forty-five [Footnote: This large proportion of the serviceable citizens, [Greek: ton en haelikia], shows the alarm at Athens. Philip's illness seems to have put a stop to his progress in Thrace at this period. Immediately on his recovery he began his aggression against Olynthus. See the Chronological Abstract prefixed to this volume.] should embark, and a tax be raised of sixty talents. That year passed; the first, second, third month arrived; in that month, reluctantly, after the mysteries, [Footnote: The Eleusinian Mysteries, in honor of Ceres and Proserpine, called The Mysteries from their peculiar sanctity.] you dispatched Charidemus with ten empty ships and five talents in money; for as Philip was reported to be sick or dead, (both rumors came.) you thought there was no longer any occasion for succors, and discontinued the armament. But that was the very occasion; if we had then sent our succors quickly, as we resolved, Philip would not have been saved to trouble us now.

Those events can not be altered. But here is the crisis of another war, the cause why I mentioned the past, that you may not repeat your error. How shall we deal with it, men of Athens? If you lend not the utmost possible aid, see how you will have manoeuvred every thing for Philip's benefit. There were the Olynthians, possessed of some power; and matters stood thus: Philip distrusted them, and they Philip. We negotiated for peace with them; this hampered (as it were) and annoyed Philip, that a great city, reconciled to us, should be watching opportunities against him. We thought it necessary by all means to make that people his enemies; and lo, what erewhile you clamored for, has somehow or other been accomplished. Then what remains, Athenians, but to assist them vigorously and promptly? I know not. For besides the disgrace that would fall upon us, if we sacrificed any of our interests, I am alarmed for the consequences, seeing how the Thebans are affected toward us, the Phocian treasury exhausted, nothing to prevent Philip, when he has subdued what lies before him, from turning to matters here. Whoever postpones until then the performance of his duty, wishes to see the peril at hand, when he may hear of it elsewhere, and to seek auxiliaries for himself, when he may be auxiliary to others; for that this will be the issue, if we throw away our present advantage, we all know pretty well.

But, it may be said, we have resolved that succors are necessary, and we will send them; tell us only how. Marvel not then, Athenians, if I say something to astonish the multitude. Appoint law-revisers: [Footnote: A provision was made by Solon for a periodical revision, of the Athenian laws by means of a legislative committee, called [Greek: Nomothetai]. See my article Nomothetes, Arch. Dict.) They were chosen by lot from the judicial body, on a reference to them by a vote of the popular assembly, Demosthenes says, "enact no statutes," instead of saying, "let the committee enact no statutes." This is because the committee would be taken from the people themselves, and the part are treated as the whole. So in speeches to juries we shall frequently observe that in mentioning the decision of some other jury he says, "you did this or that," as if they were the same persons.] at their session enact no statutes, for you have enough, but repeal those which are at present injurious; I mean, just plainly, the laws concerning our theatrical fund, and some concerning the troops, whereof the former divide the military fund among stayers-at-home for theatrical amusement, the latter indemnify deserters, and so dishearten men well inclined to the service. When you have repealed these, and made the road to good counsel safe, then find a man to propose what you all know to be desirable. But before doing so, look not for one who will advise good measures and be destroyed by you for his pains. Such a person you will not find, especially as the only result would be, for the adviser and mover to suffer wrongfully, and, without forwarding matters, to render good counsel still more dangerous in future. Besides, Athenians, you should require the same men to repeal these laws, who have introduced them. It is unjust, that their authors should enjoy a popularity which has injured the commonwealth, while the adviser of salutary measures suffers by a displeasure that may lead to general improvement. Till this is set right, Athenians, look not that any one should be so powerful with you as to transgress these laws with impunity, or so senseless as to plunge into ruin right before him.

Another thing, too, you should observe, Athenians, that a decree is worth nothing, without a readiness on your part to do what you determine. Could decrees of themselves compel you to perform your duty, or execute what they prescribe, neither would you with many decrees have accomplished little or nothing, nor would Philip have insulted you so long. Had it depended on decrees, he would have been chastised long ago. But the course of things is otherwise. Action, posterior in order of time to speaking and voting, is in efficacy prior and superior. This requisite you want; the others you possess. There are among you, Athenians, men competent to advise what is needful, and you are exceedingly quick at understanding it; ay, and you will be able now to perform it, if you act rightly. For what time or season would you have better than the present? When will you do your duty, if not now? Has not the man got possession of all our strongholds? And if he become master of this country, shall we not incur foul disgrace? Are not they, to whom we promised sure protection in case of war, at this moment in hostilities? Is he not an enemy, holding our possessions—a barbarian [Footnote: Barbarians (among the Greeks) designates persons who were not of Hellenic origin. Alexander, an ancestor of Philip, had obtained admission to the Olympic games by proving himself to be of Argive descent. But the Macedonian people were scarcely considered as Greeks till a much later period; and Demosthenes speaks rather with reference to the nation than to Philip personally.]—anything you like to call him? But, O heavens! after permitting, almost helping him to accomplish these things, shall we inquire who were to blame for them? I know we shall not take the blame to ourselves. For so in battles, no runaway accuses himself, but his general, his neighbor, any one rather; though, sure enough, the defeat is owing to all the runaways; for each one who accuses the rest might have stood his ground, and had each done so they would have conquered. Now then, does any man not give the best advice? Let another rise and give it, but not censure the last speaker. Does a second give better advice? Follow it, and success attend you! Perhaps it is not pleasant: but that is not the speaker's fault, unless he omits some needful prayer. [Footnote: Demosthenes sneers at the custom of introducing into the debate sententious professions of good-will, and prayers for prosperity; a poor substitute (he would say) for good counsel. Compare Virg. Georg. III. 454.

> Alitur vitium vivitque tegendo,
> Dum medicas adhibere manus ad vulnera pastor
> Abnegat, et meliora, Deos sedet omina poscens.]

To pray is simple enough, Athenians, collecting all that one desires in a short petition: but to decide, when measures are the subject of consideration, is not quite so easy; for we must choose the profitable rather than the pleasant, where both are not compatible.

But if any one can let alone our theatrical fund, and suggest other supplies for the military, is he not cleverer? it may be asked. I grant it, if this were possible: but I wonder if any man ever was or will be able, after wasting his means in useless expenses, to find means for useful. The wishes of men are indeed a great help to such arguments, and therefore the easiest thing in the world is self-deceit; for every man believes what he wishes, though the reality is often different. See then, Athenians, what the realities allow, and you will be able to serve and have pay. It becomes not a wise or magnanimous people, to neglect military operations for want of money, and bear disgraces like these; or, while you snatch up arms to march against Corinthians and Megarians, to let Philip enslave Greek cities for lack of provisions for your troops.

I have not spoken for the idle purpose of giving offense: I am not so foolish or perverse, as to provoke your displeasure without intending your good: but I think an upright citizen should prefer the advancement of the commonweal to the gratification of his audience. And I hear, as perhaps you do, that the speakers in our ancestors' time, whom all that address you praise, but not exactly imitate, were politicians after this form and fashion;—Aristides, Nicias, my namesake, [Footnote: Demosthenes, the general so distinguished in the Peloponnesian war, who defeated the Spartans at Pylus, and afterward lost his life in Sicily.] Pericles. But since these orators have appeared, who ask, What is your pleasure? what shall I move? how can I oblige you? the public welfare is complimented away for a moment's popularity, and these are the results; the orators thrive, you are disgraced. Mark, O Athenians, what a summary contrast may be drawn between the doings in our olden time and in yours. It is a tale brief and familiar to all; for the examples by which you may still be happy are found not abroad, men of Athens, but at home. Our forefathers, whom the speakers humored not nor caressed, as these men caress you, for five-and-forty years took the leadership of the Greeks by general consent, and brought above ten thousand talents into the citadel; and the king of this country was submissive to them, as a barbarian should be to Greeks; and many glorious trophies they erected for victories won by their own fighting on land and sea, and they are the sole people in the world who have bequeathed a renown superior to envy. Such were their merits in the affairs of Greece: see what they were at home, both as citizens and as men. Their public works are edifices and ornaments of such beauty and grandeur in temples and consecrated furniture, that posterity have no power to surpass them. In private they were so modest and attached to the principle of our constitution, that whoever knows the style of house which Aristides had, or Miltiades, and the illustrious of that day, perceives it to be no grander than those of the neighbors. Their politics were not for money-making; each felt it his duty to exalt the commonwealth. [Footnote: As Horace says:—

> Privatus illis census erat brevis,
> Commune magnum.]

By a conduct honorable toward the Greeks, pious to the gods, brotherlike among themselves, they justly attained a high prosperity.

So fared matters with them under the statesmen I have mentioned. How fare they with you under the worthies of our time? Is there any likeness or resemblance? I pass over other topics, on which I could expatiate; but observe: in this utter absence of competitors, (Lacedaemonians depressed, Thebans employed, none of the rest capable of disputing the supremacy with us,) when we might hold our own securely and arbitrate the claims of others, we have been deprived of our rightful territory, and spent above fifteen hundred talents to no purpose; the allies, whom we gained in war, these persons have lost in peace, and we have trained up against ourselves an enemy thus formidable. Or let any one come forward and tell me, by whose contrivance but ours Philip has grown strong. Well, sir, this looks bad, but things at home are better. What proof can be adduced? The parapets that are whitewashed? The roads that are repaired? fountains, and fooleries? [Footnote: Jacobs: und solches Geschwatz. The proceedings of Eubulus are here more particularly referred to.] Look at the men of whose statesmanship these are the fruits. They have risen from beggary to opulence, or from obscurity to honor; some have made their private houses more splendid than the public buildings; and in proportion as the state has declined, their fortunes have been exalted.

What has produced these results? How is it that all went prosperously then, and now goes wrong? Because anciently the people, having the courage to be soldiers, controlled the statesmen, and disposed of all emoluments; any of the rest was happy to receive from the people his share of honor, office, or advantage. Now, contrariwise, the statesmen dispose of emoluments; through them every thing is done; you the people, enervated, stripped of treasure and allies, are become as underlings and hangers-on, happy if these persons dole you out show-money or send you paltry beeves; [Footnote: Entertainments were frequently given to the people after sacrifices, at which a very small part of the victim was devoted to the gods, such as the legs and intestines, the rest being kept for more profane purposes. Tho Athenians were remarkably extravagant in sacrifices. Demades, ridiculing the donations of public meat, compared the republic to an old woman, sitting at home in slippers and supping her broth. Demosthenes, using the diminutive [Greek: boidia], charges the magistrates with supplying lean and poor oxen, whereas the victims ought to be healthy and large, [Greek: teleia]. See Virgil, Aen. xi. 739.

    Hic amor, hoc studium; dum sacra secundus aruspex
    Nuntiet, ac lucos vocet hostia pinguis in altos.]
and, the unmanliest part of all, you are grateful for receiving your own. They, cooping you in the city, lead you to your pleasures, and make you tame and submissive to their hands. It is impossible, I say, to have a high and noble spirit, while you are engaged in petty and mean employments: whatever be the pursuits of men, their characters must be similar. By Ceres, I should not wonder, if I, for mentioning these things, suffered more from your resentment than the men who have brought them to pass. For even liberty of speech you allow not on all subjects; I marvel indeed you have allowed it here.

Would you but even now, renouncing these practices, perform military service and act worthily of yourselves; would you employ these domestic superfluities as a means to gain advantage abroad; perhaps, Athenians, perhaps you might gain some solid and important advantage, and be rid of these perquisites, which are like the diet ordered by physicians for the sick. As that neither imparts strength, nor suffers the patient to die, so your allowances are not enough to be of substantial benefit, nor yet permit you to reject them and turn to something else. Thus do they increase the general apathy. What? I shall be asked: mean you stipendiary service? Yes, and forthwith the same arrangement for all, Athenians, that each, taking his dividend from the public, may be what the state requires. Is peace to be had? You are better at home, under no compulsion to act dishonorably from indigence. Is there such an emergency as the present? Better to be a soldier, as you ought, in your country's cause, maintained by those very allowances. Is any one of you beyond the military age? What he now irregularly takes without doing service, let him take by just regulation, superintending and transacting needful business. Thus, without derogating from or adding to our political system, only removing some irregularity, I bring it into order, establishing a uniform rule for receiving money, for serving in war, for sitting on juries, for doing what each according to his age can do, and what occasion requires. I never advise we should give to idlers the wages of the diligent, or sit at leisure, passive and helpless, to hear that such a one's mercenaries are victorious; as we now do. Not that I blame any one who does you a service: I only call upon you, Athenians, to perform on your own account those duties for which you honor strangers, and not to surrender that post of dignity which, won through many glorious dangers, your ancestors have bequeathed.

I have said nearly all that I think necessary. I trust you will adopt that course which is best for the country and yourselves.

THE FIRST PHILIPPIC.

THE ARGUMENT.

Philip, after the defeat of Onomarchus, had marched toward the pass of Thermopylae, which, however, he found occupied by the Athenians, who had sent a force for the purpose of preventing his advance. Being baffled there, he directed his march into Thrace, and alarmed the Athenians for the safety of their dominions in the Chersonese. At the same time he sent a fleet to attack the islands of Lemnos and Imbrus, infested the commerce of Athens with his cruisers, and even insulted her coast. In Thrace he became involved in the disputes between the rival kings Amadocus and Cersobleptes, espousing the cause of the former; and for some time he was engaged in the interior of that country, either at war with Cersobleptes, or extending his own influence over other parts of Thrace, where he established or expelled the rulers, as it suited him. It was just at that time that Demosthenes spoke the following oration, the first in which he called the attention of his countrymen to the dangerous increase of Philip's power. He had become convinced by the course of events, and by observing the restless activity of Philip, that Athens had more to fear from him than from Thebes, or from any new combination of the Grecian republics. The orator himself, perhaps, hardly appreciated the extent of Philip's resources, strengthened as he was now by the friendship of Thessaly, possessed of a navy and maritime towns, and relieved from the presence of any powerful neighbors. What were the precise views of Demosthenes as to the extent of the impending danger, we can not say. It was not for him to frighten the Athenians too much, but to awaken them from their lethargy. This he does in a speech, which, without idle declamation or useless ornament, is essentially practical. He alarms, but encourages, his countrymen; points out both their weakness and their strength; rouses them to a sense of danger, and shows the way to meet it; recommends not any extraordinary efforts, for which at the moment there was no urgent necessity, and to make which would have exceeded their power, but unfolds a scheme, simple and feasible, suiting the occasion, and calculated (if Athenians had not been too degenerate) to lay the foundation of better things.

Had the question for debate been any thing new, Athenians, I should have waited till most of the usual speakers [Footnote: By an ancient ordinance of Solon, those who were above fifty years of age were first called on to deliver their opinion. The law had ceased to be in force; but, as a decent custom, the older men usually commenced the debate. There would be frequent occasions for departing from such a custom, and Demosthenes, who was now thirty-three, assigns his reason for speaking first.] had been heard; if any of their counsels had been to my liking, I had remained silent, else proceeded to impart my own. But as the subjects of discussion is one upon which they have spoken oft before, I imagine, though I rise the first, I am entitled to indulgence. For if these men had advised properly in time past, there would be no necessity for deliberating now.

First I say, you must not despond, Athenians, under your present circumstances, wretched as they are; for that which is worst in them as regards the past, is best for the future. What do I mean? That our affairs are amiss, men of Athens, because you do nothing which is needful; if, notwithstanding you performed your duties, it were the same, there would be no hope of amendment.

Consider next, what you know by report, and men of experience remember; how vast a power the Lacedaemonians had not long ago, yet how nobly and becomingly you consulted the dignity of Athens, and undertook the war [Footnote: He refers to the war in which Athens assisted the Thebans against Lacedaemon, and in which Chabrias won the naval battle of Naxos. That war commenced twenty-six years before the speaking of the first Philippic, and would be well remembered by many of the hearers. See the Historical Abstract in this volume.] against them for the rights of Greece. Why do I mention this? To show and convince you, Athenians, that nothing, if you take precaution, is to be feared, nothing, if you are negligent, goes as you desire. Take for examples the strength of the Lacedaemonians then, which you overcame by attention to your duties, and the insolence of this man now, by which through neglect of our interests we are confounded. But if any among you, Athenians, deem Philip hard to be conquered, looking at the magnitude of his existing power, and the loss by us of all our strongholds, they reason rightly, but should reflect, that once we held Pydna and Potidaea and Methone and all the region round about as our own, and many of the nations now leagued with him were independent and free, and preferred our friendship to his. Had Philip then taken it into his head, that it was difficult to contend with Athens, when she had so many fortresses to infest his country, and he was destitute of allies, nothing that he has accomplished would he have undertaken, and never would he have acquired so large a dominion. But he saw well, Athenians, that all these places are the open prizes of war, that the possessions of the absent naturally belong to the present, those of the remiss to them that will venture and toil. Acting on such principle, he has won every thing and keeps it, either by way of conquest, or by friendly attachment and alliance; for all men will side with and respect those, whom they see prepared and willing to make proper exertion. If you, Athenians, will adopt this principle now, though you did not before, and every man, where he can and ought to give his service to the, state, be ready to give it without excuse, the wealthy to contribute, the able-bodied to enlist; in a word, plainly, if you will become your own masters, and cease each expecting to do nothing himself, while his neighbor does every thing for him, you shall then with heaven's permission recover your own, and get back what has been frittered away, and chastise Philip. Do not imagine, that his empire is everlastingly secured to him as a god. There are who hate and fear and envy him, Athenians, even among those that seem most friendly; and all feelings that are in other men belong, we may assume, to his confederates. But now they are all cowed, having no refuge through your tardiness and indolence, which I say you must abandon forthwith. For you see, Athenians, the case, to what pitch of arrogance the man has advanced, who leaves you not even the choice of action or inaction, but threatens and uses (they say) outrageous language, and, unable to rest in possession of his conquests, continually widens their circle, and, while we dally and delay, throws his net all around us. When then, Athenians, when will ye act as becomes you? In what event? In that of necessity, I suppose. And how should we regard the events happening now? Methinks, to freemen the strongest necessity is the disgrace of their condition. Or tell me, do ye like walking about and asking one another:—is there any news? Why, could there be greater news than a man of Macedonia subduing Athenians, and directing the affairs of Greece? Is Philip dead? No, but he is sick. And what matters it to you? Should any thing befall this man, you will soon create another Philip, if you attend to business thus. For even he has been exalted not so much by his own strength, as by our negligence. And again; should any thing happen to him; should fortune, which still takes better care of us than we of ourselves, be good enough to accomplish this; observe that, being on the spot, you would step in while things were in confusion, and manage them as you pleased; but as you now are, though occasion offered Amphipolis, you would not be in a position to accept it, with neither forces nor counsels at hand. [Footnote: Important advice this, to men in all relations of life. Good luck is for those who are in a position to avail themselves of it.

Illi poma cadunt qui poma sub arbore quaerit.]

However, as to the importance of a general zeal in the discharge of duty, believing you are convinced and satisfied, I say no more.

As to the kind of force which I think may extricate you from your difficulties, the amount, the supplies of money, the best and speediest method (in my judgment) of providing all the necessaries, I shall endeavor to inform you forthwith, making only one request, men of Athens. When, you have heard all, determine; prejudge not before. And let none think I delay our operations, because I recommend an entirely new force. Not those that cry, quickly! to-day! speak most to the purpose; (for what has already happened we shall not be able to prevent by our present armament;) but he that shows what and how great and whence procured must be the force capable of enduring, till either we have advisedly terminated the war, or overcome our enemies: for so shall we escape annoyance in future. This I think I am able to show, without offense to any other man who has a plan to offer. My promise indeed is large; it shall be tested by the performance; and you shall be my judges.

First, then, Athenians, I say we must provide fifty warships, [Footnote: The Athenian ship of war at this time was the Trireme, or galley with three ranks of oars. It had at the prow a beak ([Greek: embolon]), with a sharp iron head, which, in a charge, (generally made at the broadside,) was able to shatter the planks of the enemy's vessel. An ordinary trireme carried two hundred men, including the crew and marines. These last ([Greek: epibatai]) were usually ten for each ship, but the number was often increased. The transports and vessels of burden, whether merchant vessels or boats for the carriage of military stores, were round-bottomed, more bulky in construction, and moved rather with sails than oars. Hence the fighting ship is called [Greek: tacheia], swift. It carried a sail, to be used upon occasion, though it was mainly worked with oars.] and hold ourselves prepared, in case of emergency, to embark and sail. I require also an equipment of transports for half the cavalry [Footnote: The total number was one thousand, each tribe furnishing one hundred.] and sufficient boats. This we must have ready against his sudden, marches from his own country to Thermopylae, the Chersonese, Olynthus, and any where he likes. For he should entertain the belief, that possibly you may rouse from this over-carelessness, and start off, as you did to Euboea, [Footnote: The expedition about five years before, when the Thebans had sent an army to Euboea, and Timotheus roused his countrymen to expel them from the island. Of this, Demosthenes gives an animated account at the close of tho oration on the Chersonese.] and formerly (they say) to Haliartus, [Footnote: B. C. 395, when the war between Thebes and Sparta had begun and Lysander besieged Haliartus. He was slain in a sally by the Thebans and Athenians.]

and very lately to Thermopylae. And although you should not pursue just the course I would advise, it is no slight matter, that Philip, knowing you to be in readiness—know it he will for certain; there are too many among our own people who report every thing to him—may either keep quiet from apprehension, or, not heeding your arrangements, be taken off his guard, there being nothing to prevent your sailing, if he give you a chance, to attack his territories. Such an armament, I say, ought instantly to be agreed upon and provided. But besides, men of Athens, you should keep in hand some force, that will incessantly make war and annoy him: none of your ten or twenty thousand mercenaries, not your forces on paper, [Footnote: Literally "written in letters," that is, promised to the generals or allies, but never sent. Jacobs: eine Macht die auf dem Blatte steht. Compare Shakspeare, Henry IV, Second Part, Act i.

    We fortify in paper and in figures.
    Using the names of men instead of men.]
but one that shall belong to the state, and, whether you appoint one or more generals, or this or that man or any other, shall obey and follow him. Subsistence too I require for it. What the force shall be, how large, from what source maintained, how rendered efficient, I will show you, stating every particular. Mercenaries I recommend— and beware of doing what has often been injurious—thinking all measures below the occasion, adopting the strongest in your decrees, you fail to accomplish the least—rather, I say, perform and procure a little, add to it afterward, if it prove insufficient. I advise then two thousand soldiers in all, five hundred to be Athenians, of whatever age you think right, serving a limited time, not long, but such time as you think right, so as to relieve one another; the rest should be mercenaries. And with them two hundred horse, fifty at least Athenians, like the foot, on the same terms of service; and transports for them. Well; what besides? Ten swift galleys: for, as Philip has a navy, we must have swift galleys also, to convoy our power. How shall subsistence for these troops be provided? I will state and explain; but first let me tell you why I consider a force of this amount sufficient, and why I wish the men to be citizens.

    Of that amount, Athenians, because it is impossible for us now to raise an army capable of meeting him in the field: we must plunder [Footnote: Make predatory incursions, as Livy says, "popula bundi magis quam justo more belli." Jacobs: den Krieg als Freibeuter fahren. Another German: Streifzuge zu machen (guerilla warfare). Leland: "harass him with depredations." Wilson, an old English translator: "rob and spoil upon him."] and adopt such kind of warfare at first: our force, therefore, must not be over-large, (for there is not pay or subsistence,) nor altogether mean. Citizens I wish to attend and go on board, because I hear that formerly the state maintained mercenary troops at Corinth, [Footnote: He alludes to the time when Corinth, Athens, Thebes, and Argos, were allied against Sparta, and held a congress at Corinth, B. C. 394. The allies were at first defeated, but Iphicrates gained some successes, and acquired considerable reputation by cutting off a small division (mora) of Spartan infantry.] commanded by Polystratus and Iphicrates and Chabrias and some others, and that you served with them yourselves; and I am told, that these mercenaries fighting by your side and you by theirs defeated the Lacedaemonians. But ever since your hirelings have served by themselves, they have been vanquishing your friends and allies, while your enemies have become unduly great. Just glancing at the war of our state, they go off to Artabazus [Footnote: Diodorus relates that Chares, in the Social war, having no money to pay his troops, was forced to lend them to Artabazus, then in rebellion against the king of Persia. Chares gained a victory for the satrap, and received a supply of money. But this led to a complaint and menace of war by the king, which brought serious consequences. See the Historical Abstract.] or any where rather, and the general follows, naturally; for it is impossible to command without giving pay. What therefore ask I? To remove the excuses both of general and soldiers, by supplying pay, and attaching native soldiers, as inspectors of the general's conduct. The way we manage things now is a mockery. For if you were asked: Are you at peace, Athenians? No, indeed, you would say; we are at war with Philip. Did you not choose from yourselves ten captains and generals, and also captains and two generals [Footnote: There were chosen at Athens every year

> Ten generals (one for each tribe), [Greek: strataegoi].
> Ten captains (one for each tribe), [Greek: taxiarchoi].
> Two generals of cavalry, [Greek: ipparchoi].
> Ten cavalry officers (one for each tribe), [Greek: phularchoi].

In a regular army of citizens, when each tribe formed its own division, both of horse and foot, all these generals and officers would be present. Thus, there were ten generals at Marathon. A change took place in later times, when the armies were more miscellaneous. Three Athenian generals were frequently employed, and at a still later period only one. Demosthenes here touches on a very important matter, which we can well understand, viz. the necessity of officering the foreign mercenaries from home.] of horse? How are they employed? Except one man, whom you commission on service abroad, the rest conduct your processions with the sacrificers. Like puppet-makers, you elect your infantry and cavalry officers for the market-place, not for war. Consider, Athenians, should there not be native captains, a native general of horse, your own commanders, that the force might really be the state's? Or should your general of horse sail to Lemnos, [Footnote: To assist at a religious ceremony held annually at Lemnos, where many Athenians resided.] while Menelaus commands the cavalry fighting for your possessions? I speak not as objecting to the man, but he ought to be elected by you, whoever the person be.

Perhaps you admit the justice of these statements, but wish principally to hear about the supplies, what they must be and whence procured. I will satisfy you. Supplies, then, for maintenance, mere rations for these troops, come to ninety talents and a little more: for ten swift galleys forty talents, twenty minas a month to every ship; for two thousand soldiers forty more, that each soldier may receive for rations ten drachms a month; and for two hundred horsemen, each receiving thirty drachms a month, twelve talents. [Footnote: As to Athenian money, see Appendix II.] Should any one think rations for the men a small provision, he judges erroneously. Furnish that, and I am sure the army itself will, without injuring any Greek or ally, procure every thing else from the war, so as to make out their full pay. I am ready to join the fleet as a volunteer, and submit to any thing, if this be not so. Now for the ways and means of the supply, which I demand from you.

[Statement of ways and means.]

[Footnote: Here the clerk or secretary reads the scheme drawn up by Demosthenes, in the preparing of which he was probably assisted by the financial officers of the state. What follows was according to Dionysius, spoken at a different time. The curious may consult Leland, and Jacobs' introduction to his translation.]

This, Athenians, is what we have been able to devise. When you vote upon the resolutions, pass what you [Footnote: I. e. some measure, if not mine, whereby the war may be waged effectually. The reading of [Greek: poiaesate], adopted by Jacobs after Schaefer, is not in congruity with the sentence.] approve, that you may oppose Philip, not only by decrees and letters, but by action also.

I think it will assist your deliberations about the war and the whole arrangements, to regard the position, Athenians, of the hostile country, and consider, that Philip by the winds and seasons of the year gets the start in most of his operations, watching for the trade-winds [Footnote: The Etesian winds blowing from the northwest in July, which would impede a voyage from Athens to Macedonia and Thrace.] or the winter to commence them, when we are unable (he thinks) to reach the spot. On this account, we must carry on the war not with hasty levies, (or we shall be too late for every thing,) but with a permanent force and power. You may use as winter quarters for your troops Lemnos, and Thasus, and Sciathus, and the islands [Footnote: As Scopelus, Halonnesus, Peparethus, which were then subject to Athens.] in that neighborhood, which have harbors and corn and all necessaries for an army. In the season of the year, when it is easy to put ashore and there is no danger from the winds, they will easily take their station off the coast itself and at the entrances of the sea-ports.

How and when to employ the troops, the commander appointed by you will determine as occasion requires. What you must find, is stated in my bill. If, men of Athens, you will furnish the supplies which I mention, and then, after completing your preparations of soldiers, ships, cavalry, will oblige the entire force by law to remain in the service, and, while you become your own paymasters and commissaries, demand from your general an account of his conduct, you will cease to be always discussing the same questions without forwarding them in the least, and besides, Athenians, not only will you cut off his greatest revenue—What is this? He maintains war against you through the resources of your allies, by his piracies on their navigation—But what next? You will be out of the reach of injury yourselves: he will not do as in time past, when falling upon Lemnos and Imbrus he carried off your citizens captive, seizing the vessels at Geraestus he levied an incalculable sum, and lastly, made a descent at Marathon and carried off the sacred galley [Footnote: A ship called Paralus generally used on religious missions or to carry public dispatches.] from our coast, and you could neither prevent these things nor send succors by the appointed time. But how is it, think you, Athenians, that the Panathenaic and Dionysian festivals [Footnote: The Panathenaic festivals were in honor of Pallas or Athene, the protectress of Athens, and commemorated also the union of the old Attic towns under one government. There were two, the greater held every fourth year, the lesser annually. They were celebrated with sacrifices, races, gymnastic and musical contests, and various other amusements and solemnities, among which was the carrying the pictured robe of Pallas to her temple. The Dionysia, or festival of Bacchus, will be spoken of more fully hereafter.] take place always at the appointed time, whether expert or unqualified persons be chosen to conduct either of them, whereon you expend larger sums than upon any armament, and which are more numerously attended and magnificent than almost any thing in the world; while all your armaments are after the time, as that to Methone, to Pagasae, to Potidaea? Because in the former case every thing is ordered by law, and each of you knows long before-hand, who is the choir-master [Footnote: The choregus, or choir-master, of each tribe, had to defray the expense of the choruses, whether dramatic, lyric, or musical, which formed part of the entertainment on solemn occasions. This was one of the [Greek: leitourgiai], or burdensome offices, to which men of property were liable at Athens, of which we shall see more in other parts of our author.] of his tribe, who the gymnastic [Footnote: The gymnasiarch, like the choregus, had a burden imposed on him by his tribe, to make certain provisions for the gymnasium, public place or school of exercise. Some of the contests at the festivals being of a gymnastic nature, such as the Torch-race, it was his duty to make arrangements for them, and more particularly to select the ablest youths of the school for performers.] master, when, from whom, and what he is to receive, and what to do. Nothing there is left unascertained or undefined: whereas in the business of war and its preparations all is irregular, unsettled, indefinite. Therefore, no sooner have we heard any thing, than we appoint ship-captains, dispute with them on the exchanges, [Footnote: For every ship of war a captain, or trierarch, was appointed, whose duty it was, not merely to command, but take charge of the vessel, keep it in repair, and bear the expense (partly or wholly) of equipping it. In the Peloponnesian war we find the charge laid upon two joint captains, and afterward it was borne by an association formed like the Symmoriae of the Property Tax. Demosthenes, when he came to the head of affairs, introduced some useful reforms in the system of the Trierarchy.

The exchange, [Greek: antidosis], was a stringent but clumsy contrivance, to enforce the performance of these public duties by persons capable of bearing them. A party charged might call upon any other person to take take the office, or exchange estates with him. If he refused, complaint was made to the magistrate who had cognizance of the business, and the dispute was judicially heard and decided.] and consider about ways and means; then it is resolved that resident aliens and householders [Footnote: Freedmen, who had quitted their masters' house, and lived independently.] shall embark, then to put yourselves on board instead: but during these days the objects of our expedition are lost; for the time of action we waste in preparation, and favorable moments wait not our evasions and delays. The forces that we imagine we possess in the mean time, are found, when the crisis comes, utterly insufficient. And Philip has arrived at such a pitch of arrogance, as to send the following letter to the Euboeans:

[The letter is read.]

Of that which has been read, Athenians, most is true, unhappily true; perhaps not agreeable to hear. And if what one passes over in speaking, to avoid offense, one could pass over in reality, it is right to humor the audience; but if graciousness of speech, where it is out of place, does harm in action, shameful is it, Athenians, to delude ourselves, and by putting off every thing unpleasant to miss the time for all operations, and be unable even to understand, that skillful makers of war should not follow circumstances, but be in advance of them; that just as a general may be expected to lead his armies, so are men of prudent counsel to guide circumstances, in order that their resolutions may be accomplished, not their motions determined by the event. Yet you, Athenians, with larger means than any people—ships, infantry, cavalry, and revenue—have never up to this day made proper use of any of them; and your war with Philip differs in no respect from the boxing of barbarians. For among them the party struck feels always for the blow; [Footnote: Compare Virgil, Aen. ix 577.

    Ille manum projecto tegmine demens
    Ad vulnus tulit.]

strike him somewhere else, there go his hands again; ward or look in the face he can not nor will. So you, if you hear of Philip in the Chersonese, vote to send relief there if at Thermopylae, the same; if any where else, you run after his heels up and down, and are commanded by him; no plan have you devised for the war, no circumstance do you see beforehand, only [Footnote: This loose mode of expression, which is found in the original, I designedly retain.] when you learn that something is done, or about to be done. Formerly perhaps this was allowable: now it is come to a crisis, to be tolerable no longer. And it seems, men of Athens, as if some god, ashamed for us at our proceedings, has put this activity into Philip. For had he been willing to remain quiet in possession of his conquests and prizes, and attempted nothing further, some of you, I think, would be satisfied with a state of things, which brands our nation with the shame of cowardice and the foulest disgrace. But by continually encroaching and grasping after more, he may possibly rouse you, if you have not altogether despaired. I marvel, indeed, that none of you, Athenians, notices with concern and anger, that the beginning of this war was to chastise Philip, the end is to protect ourselves against his attacks. One thing is clear: he will not stop, unless some one oppose him. And shall we wait for this? And if you dispatch empty galleys and hopes from this or that person, think ye all is well? Shall we not embark? Shall we not sail with at least a part of our national forces, now though not before? Shall we not make a descent upon his coast? Where, then, shall we land? some one asks. The war itself, men of Athens, will discover the rotten parts of his empire, if we make a trial; but if we sit at home, hearing the orators accuse and malign one another, no good can ever be achieved. Methinks, where a portion of our citizens, though not all, are commissioned with the rest, Heaven blesses, and Fortune aids the struggle: but where you send out a general and an empty decree and hopes from the hustings, nothing that you desire is done; your enemies scoff, and your allies die for fear of such an armament. For it is impossible—ay, impossible, for one man to execute all your wishes: to promise, [Footnote: Chares is particularly alluded to. The "promises of Chares" passed into a proverb.] and assert, and accuse this or that person, is possible; but so your affairs are ruined. The general commands wretched unpaid hirelings; here are persons easily found, who tell you lies of his conduct; you vote at random from what you hear: what then can be expected?

How is this to cease, Athenians? When you make the same persons soldiers, and witnesses of the generals conduct, and judges when they return home at his audit; [Footnote: The audit or scrutiny of his conduct which every officer of the republic had to undergo, before a jury, if necessary, at the end of his administration. In the case of a general, the scrutiny would be like a court-martial. The Athenian people, (says Demosthenes,) as represented by the citizen soldiers, would themselves be witnesses of the general's conduct. These same soldiers, when they came home, or at least a portion of them, might serve on the jury; and so the people would be both witnesses and judges.] so that you may not only hear of your own affairs, but be present to see them. So disgraceful is our condition now, that every general is twice or thrice tried [Footnote: Chares was tried several times. Capital charges were preferred also against Autocles, Cephisodotus, Leosthenes, Callisthenes.] before you for his life, though none dares even once to hazard his life against the enemy: they prefer the death of kidnappers and thieves to that which becomes them; for it is a malefactor's part to die by sentence of the law, a general's to die in battle. Among ourselves, some go about and say that Philip is concerting with the Lacedaemonians the destruction of Thebes and the dissolution of republics; some, that he has sent envoys to the king; [Footnote: The king of Persia, generally called the king by the

Greeks.] others, that he is fortifying cities in Illyria: so we wander about, each inventing stories. For my part, Athenians, by the gods I believe, that Philip is intoxicated with the magnitude of his exploits, and has many such dreams in his imagination, seeing the absence of opponents, and elated by success; but most certainly he has no such plan of action, as to let the silliest people among us know what his intentions are; for the silliest are these newsmongers. Let us dismiss such talk, and remember only that Philip is an enemy, who robs us of our own and has long insulted us; that wherever we have expected aid from any quarter, it has been found hostile, and that the future depends on ourselves, and unless we are willing to fight him there, we shall perhaps be compelled to fight here. This let us remember, and then we shall have determined wisely, and have done with idle conjectures. You need not pry into the future, but assure yourselves it will be disastrous, unless you attend to your duty, and are willing to act as becomes you.

As for me, never before have I courted favor, by speaking what I am not convinced is for your good, and now I have spoken my whole mind frankly and unreservedly. I could have wished, knowing the advantage of good counsel to you, I were equally certain of its advantage to the counselor: so should I have spoken with more satisfaction. Now, with an uncertainty of the consequence to myself, but with a conviction that you will benefit by adopting it, I proffer my advice. I trust only, that what is most for the common benefit will prevail.

THE SECOND PHILIPPIC.

THE ARGUMENT.

Soon after the close of the Phocian war, the attention of Philip was called to Peloponnesus, where the dissensions between Sparta and her old enemies afforded him an occasion of interference. The Spartans had never abandoned their right to the province of Messenia, which had been wrested from them by Epaminondas; and since Thebes was no longer to be feared, they seem to have conceived hopes of regaining their lost power. The Argives and the Arcadians of Megalopolis were in league with Messenia, but Sparta had her allies in the Peloponnesus, and even Athens was suspected of favoring her cause. It does not appear that any open hostilities had taken place; but about this time the fears of the Messenians induced them to solicit the alliance of Philip. He willingly promised them his protection, and sent a body of troops into the Peninsula. The progress which Macedonian influence was making there having alarmed the Athenians, they sent Demosthenes with an embassy to counteract it. He went to Messene and to Argos, addressed the people, and pointed out the dangers, to which all Greece was exposed by Philip's ambition. It seems that he failed in rousing their suspicions, or they were too much occupied by an immediate peril to heed one that appeared remote. Philip however resented this proceeding on the part of the Athenians, and sent an embassy to expostulate with them, especially on the charge of bad faith and treachery which had been preferred against him by Demosthenes. Embassadors from Argos and Messene accompanied those of Macedon, and complained of the connection that appeared to subsist between Athens and Lacedaemon, hostile (they thought) to the liberties of Peloponnesus. In answer to these complaints, Demosthenes addressed his second Philippic to the Popular Assembly; repeating the substance of what he had said to the Peloponnesians, vindicating his own conduct, and denouncing the Macedonian party at Athens. The embassy led to no immediate result; but the influence of Demosthenes at home was increased.

In all the speeches, men of Athens, about Philip's measures and infringements of the peace, I observe that statements made on our behalf are thought just and generous, [Footnote: Generous, as regards the Greek states, whose independence the Athenians stand up for. This praise Demosthenes frequently claims for his countrymen, and, compared with the rest of the Greeks, they deserved it. Leland understood the word [Greek: philanthropous] in the same sense, though he translates it humane. We use the term philanthropic in a sense not unlike that of the orator; but, as Leland truly observes, "the distinction of Greek and barbarian precluded the rest of mankind from a just share in Grecian philanthropy;" and he might have added, that their notions of slavery were not in accordance with an enlarged humanity. Therefore, I prefer a word of a less arrogant meaning. Jacobs: billig. Francis: "filled with sentiments of exceeding moderation."] and all who accuse Philip are heard with approbation; yet nothing (I may say) that is proper, or for the sake of which the speeches are worth hearing, is done. To this point are the affairs of Athens brought, that the more fully and clearly one convicts Philip of violating the peace with you, and plotting against the whole of Greece, the more difficult it becomes to advise you how to act. The cause lies in all of us, Athenians, that, when we ought to oppose an ambitious power by deeds and actions, not by words, we men of the hustings [Footnote: Auger has: "nous qui montons a la tribune."] shrink from our duty of moving and advising, for fear of your displeasure, and only declaim on the heinousness and atrocity of Philip's conduct; you of the assembly, though better instructed than Philip to argue justly, or comprehend the argument of another, to check him in the execution of his designs are totally unprepared. The result is inevitable, I imagine, and perhaps just. You each succeed better in what you are busy and earnest about; Philip in actions, you in words. If you are still satisfied with using the better arguments, it is an easy matter, and there is no trouble: but if we are to take measures for the correction of these evils, to prevent their insensible progress, and the rising up of a mighty power, against which we could have no defense, then our course of deliberation is not the same as formerly; the orators, and you that hear them, must prefer good and salutary counsels to those which are easy and agreeable.

First, men of Athens, if any one regards without uneasiness the might and dominion of Philip, and imagines that it threatens no danger to the state, or that all his preparations are not against you, I marvel, and would entreat you every one to hear briefly from me the reasons, why I am led to form a contrary expectation, and wherefore I deem Philip an enemy; that, if I appear to have the clearer foresight, you may hearken to me; if they, who have such confidence and trust in Philip, you may give your adherence to them.

Thus then I reason, Athenians. What did Philip first make himself master of after the peace? Thermopylae and the Phocian state. Well, and how used he his power? He chose to act for the benefit of Thebes, not of Athens. Why so? Because, I conceive, measuring his calculations by ambition, by his desire of universal empire, without regard to peace, quiet, or justice, he saw plainly, that to a people of our character and principles nothing could he offer or give, that would induce you for self-interest to sacrifice any of the Greeks to him. He sees that you, having respect for justice, dreading the infamy of the thing, and exercising proper forethought, would oppose him in any such attempt as much as if you were at war: but the Thebans he expected (and events prove him right) would, in return for the services done them, allow him in every thing else to have his way, and, so far from thwarting or impeding him, would fight on his side if he required it. From the same persuasion he befriended lately the Messenians and Argives, which is the highest panegyric upon you, Athenians; for you are adjudged by these proceedings to be the only people incapable of betraying for lucre the national rights of Greece, or bartering your attachment to her for any obligation or benefit. And this opinion of you, that (so different) of the Argives and Thebans, he has naturally formed, not only from a view of present times, but by reflection on the past. For assuredly he finds and hears that your ancestors, who might have governed the rest of Greece on terms of submitting to Persia, not only spurned the proposal, when Alexander, [Footnote: Alexander of Macedon, son of Amyntas, was sent by Mardonius, the Persian commander, to offer the most favorable terms to the Athenians, if they would desert the cause of the Greeks. The Spartans at the same time sent an embassy, to remind them of their duty. The spirited reply which the Athenians made to both embassies is related by Herodotus. The Thebans submitted to Xerxes, and fought against the Greeks at the battle of Plataea. The Argives were neutral, chiefly from jealousy of Sparta. They demanded half the command of the allied army, as a condition of their assistance, but this could not be complied with.] this man's ancestor, came as herald to negotiate, but preferred to abandon their country and endure any suffering, and thereafter achieved such exploits as all the world loves to mention, though none could ever speak them worthily, and therefore I must be silent; for their deeds are too mighty to be uttered [Footnote: The simple [Greek: eipein] in the original is more forcible than if it had been [Greek: epainein], or the like. Compare Shakspeare, Coriolanus, Act ii. sc. 2.

> I shall lack voice: the deeds of Coriolanus
> Should not be uttered feebly——
>   For this last
> Before and in Corioli, let me say,
> I can not speak him home.]

in words. But the forefathers of the Argives and Thebans, they either joined the barbarian's army, or did not oppose it; and therefore he knows that both will selfishly embrace their advantage, without considering the common interest of the Greeks. He thought then, if he chose your friendship, it must be on just principles; if he attached himself to them he should find auxiliaries of his ambition. This is the reason of his preferring them to you both then and now. For certainly he does not see them with a larger navy than you, nor has he acquired an inland empire and renounced that of the sea and the ports, nor does he forget the professions and promises on which he obtained the peace.

Well, it may be said, he knew all this, yet he so acted, not from ambition or the motives which I charge, but because the demands of the Thebans were more equitable than yours. Of all pleas, this now is the least open to him. He that bids the Lacedaemonians resign Messene, how can he pretend, when he delivered Orchomenos and Coronea to the Thebans, to have acted on a conviction of justice?

But, forsooth, he was compelled,—this plea remains—he made concessions against his will, being surrounded by Thessalian horse and Theban infantry. Excellent! So of his intentions they talk; he will mistrust the Thebans; and some carry news about, that he will fortify Elatea. All this he intends and will intend I dare say; but to attack the Lacedaemonians on behalf of Messene and Argos he does not intend; he actually sends mercenaries and money into the country, and is expected himself with a great force. The

Lacedaemonians, who are enemies of Thebes, he overthrows; the Phocians, whom he himself before destroyed, will he now preserve?

And who can believe this? I can not think that Philip, either if he was forced into his former measures, or if he were now giving up the Thebans, would pertinaciously oppose their enemies; his present conduct rather shows that he adopted those measures by choice. All things prove to a correct observer, that his whole plan of action is against our state. And this has now become to him a sort of necessity. Consider. He desires empire: he conceives you to be his only opponents. He has been for some time wronging you, as his own conscience best informs him, since, by retaining what belongs to you, he secures the rest of his dominion: had he given up Amphipolis and Potidaea, he deemed himself unsafe at home. He knows therefore, both that he is plotting against you, and that you are aware of it; and, supposing you to have intelligence, he thinks you must hate him; he is alarmed, expecting some disaster, if you get the chance, unless he hastes to prevent you. Therefore he is awake, and on the watch against us; he courts certain people, Thebans, and people in Peloponnesus of the like views, who from cupidity, he thinks, will be satisfied with the present, and from dullness of understanding will foresee none of the consequences. And yet men of even moderate sense might notice striking facts, which I had occasion to quote to the Messenians and Argives, and perhaps it is better they should be repeated to you.

Ye, men of Messene, said I, how do ye think the Olynthians would have brooked to hear any thing against Philip at those times, when he surrendered to them Anthemus, which all former kings of Macedonia claimed, when he cast out the Athenian colonists and gave them Potidaea, taking on himself your enmity, and giving them the land to enjoy? Think ye they expected such treatment as they got, or would have believed it if they had been told? Nevertheless, said I, they, after enjoying for a short time the land of others, are for a long time deprived by him of their own, shamefully expelled, not only vanquished, but betrayed by one another and sold. In truth, these too close connections with despots are not safe for republics. The Thessalians, again, think ye, said I, when he ejected their tyrants, and gave back Nicaea and Magnesia, they expected to have the decemvirate [Footnote: Thessaly was anciently divided into four districts, each called a tetras, and this, as we learn from the third Philippic, was restored soon after the termination of the Sacred war. The object of Philip in effecting this arrangement was, no doubt, to weaken the influence of the great Thessalian families by a division of power; otherwise the Pheraean tyranny might have been exchanged for an oligarchy powerful enough to be independent of Macedonia. The decemvirate here spoken of (if the text be correct) was a further contrivance to forward Philip's views; whether we adopt Leland's opinion, that each tetrarchy was governed by a council of ten, or Schaefer's, that each city was placed under ten governors. Jacobs understands the word decemvirate not to refer to any positive form of government, but generally to designate a tyranny, such as that which the Lacedaemonians used to introduce into conquered cities. So, for example, the Romans might have spoken of a decemvirate after the time of Appius. However this be, Philip seems to have contrived that the ruling body, whether in the tetrarchy or the decadarchy, should be his own creatures. Two of them, Eudicus and Simus, are particularly mentioned by Demosthenes as traitors.] which is now established? or that he who restored the meeting at Pylae [Footnote: Pylae, which signifies gates, was a name applied by the Greeks to divers passes, or defiles, but especially to the pass of Thermopylae, which opened through the ridges of Mount Oeta into the country of the

Epicnemidian Locrians, and was so called from the hot sulphureous springs that gushed from the foot of the mountain.] would take away their revenues? Surely not. And yet these things have occurred, as all mankind may know. You behold Philip, I said, a dispenser of gifts and promises: pray, if you are wise, that you may never know him for a cheat and a deceiver. By Jupiter, I said, there are manifold contrivances for the guarding and defending of cities, as ramparts, walls, trenches, and the like: these are all made with hands, and require expense; but there is one common safeguard in the nature of prudent men, which is a good security for all, but especially for democracies against despots. What do I mean? Mistrust. Keep this, hold to this; preserve this only, and you can never be injured. What do ye desire? Freedom. Then see ye not that Philip's very titles are at variance therewith? Every king and despot is a foe to freedom, an antagonist to laws. Will ye not beware, I said, lest, seeking deliverance from war, you find a master?

They heard me with a tumult of approbation; and many other speeches they heard from the ambassadors, both in my presence and afterward; yet none the more, as it appears, will they keep aloof from Philip's friendship and promises. And no wonder, that Messenians and certain Peloponnesians should act contrary to what their reason approves; but you, who understand yourselves, and by us orators are told, how you are plotted against, how you are inclosed! you, I fear, to escape present exertion, will come to ruin ere you are aware. So doth the moment's case and indulgence prevail over distant advantage.

As to your measures, you will in prudence, I presume, consult hereafter by yourselves. I will furnish you with such an answer as it becomes the assembly to decide upon.

[Here the proposed answer was read]

[Footnote: Whether this was moved by the orator himself, or formally read as his motion by the officer of the assembly, does not appear.]

It were just, men of Athens, to call the persons who brought those promises, on the faith whereof you concluded peace. For I should never have submitted to go as ambassador, and you would certainly not have discontinued the war, had you supposed that Philip, on obtaining peace, would act thus; but the statements then made were very different. Ay, and others you should call. Whom? The men who declared—after the peace, when I had returned from my second mission, that for the oaths—when, perceiving your delusion, I gave warning, and protested, and opposed the abandonment of Thermopylae and the Phocians—that I, being a water-drinker, [Footnote: It was Philocrates who said this. There were many jokes against Demosthenes as a water-drinker.] was naturally a churlish and morose fellow, that Philip, if he passed the straits, would do just as you desired, fortify Thespiae and Plataea, humble the Thebans, cut through the Chersonese [Footnote: This peninsula being exposed to incursions from Thrace, a plan was conceived of cutting through the isthmus from Pteleon to Leuce-Acte, to protect the Athenian settlements. See the Appendix to this volume, on the Thracian Chersonese.] at his own expense, and give you Oropus and Euboea in exchange for Amphipolis. All these declarations on the hustings I am sure you remember, though you are not famous for remembering injuries. And, the most disgraceful thing of all, you voted in your confidence, that this same peace should descend to your posterity; so completely were you misled. Why mention I this now, and desire these men to be called? By the gods,

I will tell you the truth frankly and without reserve. Not that I may fall a-wrangling, to provoke recrimination before you, [Footnote: Similarly Auger: "Ce n'est pas pour m'attirer les invectives de mes anciens adversaires en les invectivant moi-meme." Jacobs otherwise: Nicht um durch Schmahungen mir auf gleiche Weise Gehor bei Euch zu verschaffen. But I do not think that [Greek: emauto logon poiaeso] can bear the sense of [Greek: logon tuchoimi], "get a hearing for myself." And the orator's object is, not so much to sneer at the people by hinting that they are ready to hear abuse, as to deter his opponents from retaliation, or weaken its effect, by denouncing their opposition as corrupt. Leland saw the meaning: "Not that, by breaking out into invectives, I may expose myself to the like treatment."] and afford my old adversaries a fresh pretext for getting more from Philip, nor for the purpose of idle garrulity. But I imagine that what Philip is doing will grieve you hereafter more than it does now. I see the thing progressing, and would that my surmises were false; but I doubt it is too near already. So when you are able no longer to disregard events, when, instead of hearing from me or others that these measures are against Athens, you all see it yourselves, and know it for certain, I expect you will be wrathful and exasperated. I fear then, as your embassadors have concealed the purpose for which they know they were corrupted, those who endeavor to repair what the others have lost may chance to encounter your resentment; for I see it is a practice with many to vent their anger, not upon the guilty, but on persons most in their power. While therefore the mischief is only coming and preparing, while we hear one another speak, I wish every man, though he knows it well, to be reminded, who it was [Footnote: He means Aeschines.] persuaded you to abandon Phocis and Thermopylae, by the command of which Philip commands the road to Attica and Peloponnesus, and has brought it to this, that your deliberation must be, not about claims and interests abroad, but concerning the defense of your home and a war in Attica, which will grieve every citizen when it comes, and indeed it has commenced from that day. Had you not been then deceived, there would be nothing to distress the state. Philip would certainly never have prevailed at sea and come to Attica with a fleet, nor would he have marched with a land-force by Phocis and Thermopylae: he must either have acted honorably, observing the peace and keeping quiet, or been immediately in a war similar to that which made him desire the peace. Enough has been said to awaken recollection. Grant, O ye gods, it be not all fully confirmed! I would have no man punished, though death he may deserve, to the damage and danger of the country.

THE THIRD PHILIPPIC.

THE ARGUMENT.

This speech was delivered about three months after the last, while Philip was advancing into Thrace, and threatening both the Chersonese and the Propontine coast. No new event had happened, which called for any special consultation; but Demosthenes, alarmed by the formidable character of Philip's enterprises and vast military preparations, felt the necessity of rousing the Athenians to exertion. He repeats in substance the arguments which he had used in the Oration on the Chersonese; points out the danger to be apprehended from the disunion among the Greek states, from their general apathy and lack of patriotism, which he contrasts with the high and noble spirit of ancient times. From the past conduct of Philip he shows what is to be expected in future; explains the difference between Philip's new method of warfare and that adopted in the Peloponnesian war, and urges the necessity of corresponding measures for defense. The peaceful professions of Philip were not to be trusted; he was never more dangerous than when he made overtures of peace and friendship. The most powerful instruments that he employed for gaining ascendency were the venal orators, who were to be found in every Grecian city, and on whom it was necessary to inflict signal punishment, before they had a chance of opposing foreign enemies. The advice of Demosthenes now is, to dispatch reinforcements to the Chersonese, to stir up the people of Greece, and even to solicit the assistance of the Persian king, who had no less reason than themselves to dread the ambition of Philip.

The events of the following year, when Philip attacked the Propontine cities, fully justified the warning of Demosthenes. And the extraordinary activity, which the Athenians displayed in resisting him, shows that the exertions of the orator had their due effect. Even Mitford confesses, with reference to the operations of that period, that Athens found in Demosthenes an able and effective minister.

Many speeches, men of Athens, are made in almost every assembly about the hostilities of Philip, hostilities which ever since the treaty of peace he has been committing as well against you as against the rest of the Greeks; and all (I am sure) are ready to avow, though they forbear to do so, that our counsels and our measures should be directed to his humiliation and chastisement: nevertheless, so low have our affairs been brought by inattention and negligence, I fear it is a harsh truth to say, that if all the orators had sought to suggest, and you to pass resolutions for the utter ruining of the commonwealth, we could not methinks be worse off than we are. A variety of circumstances may have brought us to this state; our affairs have not declined from one or two causes only; but, if you rightly examine, you will find it chiefly owing to the orators, who study to please you rather than advise for the best. Some of whom, Athenians, seeking to maintain the basis of their own power and repute, have no forethought for the future, and therefore think you also ought to have none; others, accusing and calumniating practical statesmen, labor only to make Athens punish Athens, and in such occupations to engage her, that Philip may have liberty to say and do what he pleases. Politics of this kind are common here, but are the causes of your failures and embarrassment. I beg, Athenians, that you will not resent my plain speaking of the truth. Only consider. You hold liberty of speech in other matters to be the general right of all residents in Athens, insomuch that you allow a measure of it even to foreigners and slaves, and many servants may be seen among you speaking their thoughts more freely than citizens in some other states; and yet you have altogether banished it from your councils. The result has been, that in the assembly you give yourselves airs and are flattered at hearing nothing but compliments, in your measures and proceedings you are brought to the utmost peril. If such be your disposition now, I must be silent: if you will listen to good advice without flattery, I am ready to speak. For though our affairs are in a deplorable condition, though many sacrifices have been made, still, if you will choose to perform your duty, it is possible to repair it all. A paradox, and yet a truth, am I about to state. That which is the most lamentable in the past is best for the future. How is this? Because you performed no part of your duty, great or small, and therefore you fared ill: had you done all that became you, and your situation were the same, there would be no hope of amendment. Philip has indeed prevailed over your sloth and negligence, but not over the country: you have not been worsted; you have not even bestirred yourselves.

If now we were all agreed that Philip is at war with Athens and infringing the peace, nothing would a speaker need to urge or advise but the safest and easiest way of resisting him. But since, at the very time when Philip is capturing cities and retaining divers of our dominions and assailing all people, there are men so unreasonable as to listen to repeated declarations in the assembly, that some of us are kindling war, one must be cautious and set this matter right: for whoever moves or advises a measure of defense, is in danger of being accused afterward as author of the war.

I will first then examine and determine this point, whether it be in our power to deliberate on peace or war. If the country may be at peace, if it depends on us, (to begin with this,) I say we ought to maintain peace, and I call upon the affirmant to move a resolution, to take some measure, and not to palter with us. But if another, having arms in his hand and a large force around him, amuses you with the name of peace, while he carries on the operations of war, what is left but to defend yourselves? You may profess to be at peace, if you like, as he does; I quarrel not with that. But if any man supposes this to be a peace, which will enable Philip to master all else and attack you last, he is a madman, or he talks of a peace observed toward him by you, not toward you by him. This it is that Philip purchases by all his expenditure, the privilege of assailing you without being assailed in turn.

If we really wait until he avows that he is at war with us, we are the simplest of mortals, for he would not declare that, though he marched even against Attica and Piraeus, at least if we may judge from his conduct to others. For example, to the Olynthians he declared, when he was forty furlongs from their city, that there was no alternative, but either they must quit Olynthus or he Macedonia; though before that time, whenever he was accused of such an intent, he took it ill and sent embassadors to justify himself. Again, he marched towards the Phocions as if they were allies, and there were Phocian envoys who accompanied his march, and many among you contended that his advance would not benefit the Thebans. And he came into Thessaly of late as a friend and ally, yet he has taken possession of Pherae: and lastly he told these wretched people of Oreus, [Footnote: When he established his creature Philistides in the government of Oreus, as mentioned in the last oration and at the end of this.] that he had sent his soldiers out of good-will to visit them, as he heard they were in trouble and dissension, and it was the part of allies and true friends to lend assistance on such occasions. People who would never have harmed him, though they might have adopted measures of defense, he chose to deceive rather than warn them of his attack; and think ye he would declare war against you before he began it, and that while you are willing to be deceived? Impossible. He would be the silliest of mankind, if, while you the injured parties make no complaint against him, but are accusing your own countrymen, he should terminate your intestine strife and jealousies, warn you to turn against him, and remove the pretexts of his hirelings for asserting, to amuse you, that he makes no war upon Athens. O heavens! would any rational being judge by words rather than by actions, who is at peace with him and who at war? Surely none. Well then; Philip immediately after the peace, before Diopithes was in command or the settlers in the Chersonese had been sent out, took Serrium and Doriscus, and expelled from Serrium and the Sacred Mount the troops whom your general had stationed there. [Footnote: This general was Chares, to whom Cersobleptes had intrusted the defense of those places. The Sacred Mount was a fortified position on the northern coast of the Hellespont. It was here that Miltocythes intrenched himself, when he rebelled against Cotys; and Philip took possession of it just before the peace with Athens was concluded, as being important to his operations against Cersobleptes. The statement of Demosthenes, that the oaths had then been taken, is, as Jacobs observes, incorrect; for they were sworn afterward in Thessaly. But the argument is substantially the same, for the peace had been agreed to, and the ratification was purposely delayed by Philip, to gain time for the completion of his designs.] What do you call such conduct? He had sworn the peace. Don't say—what does it signify? how is the state concerned?—Whether it be a trifling matter, or of no concernment to you, is a different question: religion and justice have the same obligation, be the subject of the offense great or small. Tell me now; when he sends mercenaries into Chersonesus, which the king and all the Greeks have acknowledged to be yours, when he avows himself an auxiliary and writes us word so, what are such proceedings? He says he is not at war; I can not however admit such conduct to be an observance of the peace; far otherwise: I say, by his attempt on Megara, [Footnote: Not long before this oration was delivered, Philip was suspected of a design to seize Megara. Demosthenes gives an account, in his speech on the Embassy, of a conspiracy between two Megarians, Ptaeodorus and Perilaus, to introduce Macedonian troops into the city. Phocion was sent by the Athenians to Megara, with the consent of the Megarian people, to protect them against foreign attack. He fortified the city and port, connecting them by long walls, and put them in security. The occupation of Megara by Philip must have been most perilous to Athens, especially while Euboea and Thebes were in his interest; he would thus have inclosed her as it were in a net.] by his setting up despotism in Euboea, by his present advance into Thrace, by his intrigues in Peloponnesus, by the whole course of operations with his army, he has been breaking the peace and making war upon you; unless indeed you will say, that those who establish batteries are not at war, until they apply them to the walls. But that you will not say: for whoever contrives and prepares the means for my conquest, is at war with me, before he darts or draws the bow. What, if any thing should happen, is the risk you run? The alienation of the Hellespont, the subjection of Megara and Euboea to your enemy, the siding of the Peloponnesians with him. Then can I allow, that one who sets such an engine at work against Athens is at peace with her? Quite the contrary. From the day that he destroyed the Phocians I date his commencement of hostilities. Defend yourselves instantly, and I say you will be wise: delay it, and you may wish in vain to do so hereafter. So much do I dissent from your other counselors, men of Athens, that I deem any discussion about Chersonesus or Byzantium out of place. Succor them—I advise that— watch that no harm befalls them, send all necessary supplies to your troops in that quarter; but let your deliberations be for the safety of all Greece, as being in the utmost peril. I must tell you why I am so alarmed at the state of our affairs: that, if my reasonings are correct, you may share them, and make some provision at least for yourselves, however disinclined to do so for others: but if, in your judgment, I talk nonsense and absurdity, you may treat me as crazed, and not listen to me, either now or in future.

That Philip from a mean and humble origin has grown mighty, that the Greeks are jealous and quarreling among themselves, that it was far more wonderful for him to rise from that insignificance, than it would now be, after so many acquisitions, to conquer what is left; these and similar matters, which I might dwell upon, I pass over. But I observe that all people, beginning with you, have conceded to him a right, which in former times has been the subject of contest in every Grecian war. And what is this? The right of doing what he pleases, openly fleecing and pillaging the Greeks, one after another, attacking and enslaving their cities. You were at the head of the Greeks for seventy-three years, [Footnote: This would be from about the end of the Persian war to the end of the

Peloponnesian, B. C. 405. Isocrates speaks of the Athenian sway as having lasted sixty-five or seventy years. But statements of this kind are hardly intended to be made with perfect accuracy. In the third Olynthiac, as we have seen, Demosthenes says, the Athenians had the leadership by consent of the Greeks for forty-five years. This would exclude the Peloponnesian war.] the Lacedaemonians for twenty-nine; [Footnote: From the end of the Peloponnesian war to the battle of Naxos, B. C. 376.] and the Thebans had some power in these latter times after the battle of Leuctra. Yet neither you, my countrymen, nor Thebans nor Lacedaemonians, were ever licensed by the Greeks to act as you pleased; far otherwise. When you, or rather the Athenians at that time, appeared to be dealing harshly with certain people, all the rest, even such as had no complaint against Athens, thought proper to side with the injured parties in a war against her. So, when the Lacedaemonians became masters and succeeded to your empire, on their attempting to encroach and make oppressive innovations, [Footnote: The Spartans, whose severe military discipline rendered them far the best soldiers in Greece, were totally unfit to manage the empire, at the head of which they found themselves after the humiliation of Athens. Their attempt to force an oligarchy upon every dependent state was an unwise policy, which made them generally odious. The decemvirates of Lysander, and the governors ([Greek: armostai]) established in various Greek cities to maintain Lacedaemonian influence, were regarded as instruments of tyranny. It was found that Spartan governors and generals, when away from home, gave loose to their vicious inclinations, as if to indemnify themselves for the strictness of domestic discipline. It became a maxim in their politics, that the end justified the means. The most flagrant proof was given by the seizure of the Cadmea at Thebes; a measure, which led to a formidable confederacy against Sparta, and brought her to the verge of destruction.] a general war was declared against them, even by such as had no cause of complaint. But wherefore mention other people? We ourselves and the Lacedaemonians, although at the outset we could not allege any natural injuries, thought proper to make war for the injustice that we saw done to our neighbors. Yet all the faults committed by the Spartans in those thirty years, and by our ancestors in the seventy, are less, men of Athens, than the wrongs which, in thirteen incomplete years that Philip has been uppermost, [Footnote: I. e. in power; but, as Smead, an American editor, truly observes, [Greek: epipolyxei] has a contemptuous signification, Jacobs: oben schwimmt. The thirteen years are reckoned from the time when Philip's interference in Thessaly began; before which he had not assumed an important character in southern Greece.] he has inflicted on the Greeks: nay they are scarcely a fraction of these, as may easily be shown in a few words. Olynthus and Methone and Apollonia, and thirty-two cities [Footnote: The Chalcidian cities.] on the borders of Thrace, I pass over; all which he has so cruelly destroyed, that a visitor could hardly tell if they were ever inhabited: and of the Phocians, so considerable a people exterminated, I say nothing. But what is the condition of Thessaly? Has he not taken away her constitutions and her cities, and established tetrarchies, to parcel her out, [Footnote: This statement does not disagree with the mention of the [Greek: dekadarchia] in the second Philippic. Supposing that Thessaly was not only divided into tetrarchics, four provinces or cantons, but also governed by decemvirates of Philip's appointment, placed in divers of her cities, then by the former contrivance she might be said [Greek: donlenein kat ethnae], by the latter [Greek: kata poleis]. It is not clear indeed whether several decemvirates, or one for the whole country, is to be understood. The singular number is equally capable of either interpretation.] not only by cities, but also by provinces, for subjection? Are not the Euboean states governed now by despots, and that in an island near to Thebes and Athens? Does he not expressly write in his epistles, "I am at peace with those who are willing to obey me?" Nor does he write so and not act accordingly. He is gone to the Hellespont; he marched formerly against Ambracia; Elis, such an important city in Peloponnesus, he possesses; [Footnote: That is to say; a Macedonian faction prevailed in Elis. The democratical party had some time before endeavored to regain the ascendency, by aid of the Phocian mercenaries of Phalaecus; but they had been defeated by the troops of Arcadia and Elis.] he plotted lately to get Megara: neither Hellenic nor Barbaric land contains the man's ambition. [Footnote: So Juvenal, Sat X. 160:

Aestuat infelix angusto limite mundi,
 Ut Gyarae clausus scopulis parvaque Seripho.
And Virgil, Aen. IX. 644:

Nee te Troja capit.]

And we the Greek community, seeing and hearing this, instead of sending embassies to one another about it and expressing indignation, are in such a miserable state, so intrenched in our miserable towns, that to this day we can attempt nothing that interest or necessity requires; we can not combine, or form any association for succor and alliance; we look unconcernedly on the man's growing power, each resolving (methinks) to enjoy the interval that another is destroyed in, not caring or striving for the salvation of Greece: for none can be ignorant, that Philip, like some course or attack of fever or other disease, is coming even on those that yet seem very far removed. And you must be sensible, that whatever wrong the Greeks sustained from Lacedaemonians or from us, was at least inflicted by genuine people of Greece; and it might be felt in the same manner as if a lawful son, born to a large fortune, committed some fault or error in the management of it; on that ground one would consider him open to censure and reproach, yet it could not be said that he was an alien, and not heir to the property which he so dealt with. But if a slave or a spurious child wasted and spoiled what he had no interest in—Heavens! how much more heinous and hateful would all have pronounced it! And yet in regard to Philip and his conduct they feel not this, although he is not only no Greek and noway akin to Greeks, but not even a barbarian of a place honorable to mention; in fact, a vile fellow of Macedon, from which a respectable slave could not be purchased formerly.

What is wanting to make his insolence complete? Besides his destruction of Grecian cities, does he not hold the Pythian games, the common festival of Greece, and, if he comes not himself, send his vassals to preside? Is he not master of Thermopylae and the passes into Greece, and holds he not those places by garrisons and mercenaries? Has he not thrust aside Thessalians, ourselves, Dorians, the whole Amphictyonic body, and got preaudience of the oracle, [Footnote: This privilege, which had belonged to the Phocians, was transferred to Philip. It was considered an advantage as well as an honor in ancient times; for there were only certain days appointed in every month, when the oracle could be consulted, and the order of consultation was determined by lot in common cases. The Delphians used to confer the right of pre-consultation on particular states or persons as a reward for some service or act of piety. Thus the Spartans received it; and Croesus, king of Lydia, for the magnificent presents which he sent to the temple.] to which even the Greeks do not all pretend? Does he not write to the Thessalians, what form of government to adopt? send mercenaries to Porthmus, [Footnote: Porthmus was the port of Eretria, on the strait, opposite Athens. The circumstances are stated by Demosthenes at the latter end of the speech. By expelling the [Greek: daemos] of Eretria, he means of course the popular party, die Volkspartei, as Pabst has it; but they would by their own partisans be called the people.] to expel the Eretrian commonalty; others to Oreus, to set up Philistides as ruler? Yet the Greeks endure to see all this; methinks they view it as they would a hailstorm, each praying that it may not fall on himself, none trying to prevent it. And not only are the outrages which he does to Greece submitted to, but even the private wrongs of every people: nothing can go beyond this! Has he not wronged the Corinthians by attacking Ambracia [Footnote: Divers colonies were planted on the northwestern coast of Greece by the Corinthians, and also by the Coreyraeans, who were themselves colonists from Corinth. Among them were Leucas, Ambracia, Anactorium, Epidamnus, and Apollonia. Leucas afterward became insular, by cutting through the isthmus. Philip's meditated attack was in 343 B. C. after the conquest of Cassopia. Leucas, by its insular position, would have been convenient for a descent on Peloponnesus. We have seen that this design of Philip was baffled by the exertions of Demosthenes.] and Leucas? the Achaians, by swearing to give Naupactus [Footnote: Naupactus, now Lepanto, lay on the northern coast of the Corinthian gulf. At the close of the Peloponnesian war it came into the hands of the Achaians, from whom it was taken by Epaminondas, but after his death they regained it. The Aetolians got possession of the town some time after, perhaps by Macedonian assistance.] to the Aetolians? from the Thebans taken Echinus? [Footnote: The Echinus here mentioned was a city on the northern coast of the Maliac gulf in Thessaly.] Is he not marching against the Byzantines his allies? From us—I omit the rest—but keeps he not Cardia, the greatest city of the Chersonese? Still under these indignities we are all slack and disheartened, and look toward our neighbors, distrusting one another, instead of the common enemy. And how think ye a man, who behaves so insolently to all, how will he act, when he gets each separately under his control?

But what has caused the mischief? There must be some cause, some good reason, why the Greeks were so eager for liberty then, and now are eager for servitude. There was something, men of Athens, something in the hearts of the multitude then, which there is not now, which overcame the wealth of Persia and maintained the freedom of Greece, and quailed not under any battle by land or sea; the loss whereof has ruined all, and thrown the affairs of Greece into confusion. What was this? Nothing subtle or clever: simply that whoever took money from the aspirants for power or the corruptors of Greece were universally detested: it was dreadful to be convicted of bribery; the severest punishment was inflicted on the guilty, and there was no intercession or pardon. The favorable moments for enterprise, which fortune frequently offers to the careless against the vigilant, to them that will do nothing against those that discharge all their duty, could not be bought from orators or generals; no more could mutual concord, nor distrust of tyrants and barbarians, nor any thing of the kind. But now all such principles have been sold as in open market, and those imported in exchange, by which Greece is ruined and diseased. [Footnote: [Greek: Apolole] in reference to foreign affairs; [Greek: nenosaeken] in regard to internal broils and commotions. Compare Shakspeare, Macbeth IV. 8.

O nation miserable,
When shalt thou see thy wholesome days again?]
What are they? Envy where a man gets a bribe; laughter if he confesses it; mercy to the convicted; hatred of those that denounce the crime: all the usual attendants upon corruption. [Footnote: He glances more particularly at Philocrates, Demades, and Aeschines.] For as to ships and men and revenues and abundance of other materials, all that may be reckoned as constituting national strength—assuredly the Greeks of our day

are more fully and perfectly supplied with such advantages than Greeks of the olden time. But they are all rendered useless, unavailable, unprofitable, by the agency of these traffickers.

That such is the present state of things, you must see, without requiring my testimony: that it was different in former times, I will demonstrate, not by speaking my own words, but by showing an inscription of your ancestors, which they graved on a brazen column and deposited in the citadel, not for their own benefit, (they were right-minded enough without such records,) but for a memorial and example to instruct you, how seriously such conduct should be taken up. What says the inscription then? It says: "Let Arthmius, son of Pythonax the Zelite, [Footnote: Zelea is a town in Mysia. Arthmius was sent by Artaxerxes into Peloponnesus, to stir up a war against the Athenians, who had irritated him by the assistance which they lent to Egypt. Aeschines says that Arthmius was the [Greek: proxenos] of Athens, which may partly account for the decree passed against him.] be declared an outlaw, [Footnote: Of the various degrees of [Greek: atimia] at Athens I shall speak hereafter. I translate the word here, so as to meet the case of a foreigner, who had nothing to do with the franchises of the Athenians, but who by their decree was excommunicated from the benefit of all international law.] and an enemy of the Athenian people and their allies, him and his family." Then the cause is written why this was done: because he brought the Median gold into Peloponnesus. That is the inscription. By the gods! only consider and reflect among yourselves, what must have been the spirit, what the dignity of those Athenians who acted so! One Arthmius a Zelite, subject of the king, (for Zelea is in Asia,) because in his master's service he brought gold into Peloponnesus, not to Athens, they proclaimed an enemy of the Athenians and their allies, him and his family, and outlawed. That is, not the outlawry commonly spoken of: for what would a Zelite care, to be excluded from Athenian franchises? It means not that; but in the statutes of homicide it is written, in cases where a prosecution for murder is not allowed, but killing is sanctioned, "and let him die an outlaw," says the legislator: by which he means, that whoever kills such a person shall be unpolluted. [Footnote: That is, his act being justifiable homicide, he shall not be deemed (in a religious point of view) impure. As to the Athenian law of homicide, see my article Phonos in the Archaeological Dictionary.] Therefore they considered that the preservation of all Greece was their own concern: (but for such opinion, they would not have cared, whether people in Peloponnesus were bought and corrupted:) and whomsoever they discovered taking bribes, they chastised and punished so severely as to record their names in brass. The natural result was, that Greece, was formidable to the Barbarian, not the Barbarian to Greece. 'Tis not so now: since neither in this nor in other respects are your sentiments the same. But what are they? You know yourselves: why am I to upbraid you with every thing? The Greeks in general are alike and no better than you. Therefore I say, our present affairs demand earnest attention and wholesome counsel. Shall I say what? Do you bid me, and won't you be angry?

[Here is read the public document which Demosthenes produces, after which he resumes his address.]

[Footnote: The Secretary of the Assembly stood by the side of the orator, and read any public documents, such as statutes, decrees, bills and the like, which the orator desired to refer to or to verify. It does not appear what the document was, which Demosthenes caused to be read here. If we may judge from the argument, it was some energetic resolution of the people, such as he would propose for an example on the present occasion.]

There is a foolish saying of persons who wish to make us easy, that Philip is not yet as powerful as the Lacedaemonians were formerly, who ruled every where by land and sea, and had the king for their ally, and nothing withstood them; yet Athens resisted even that nation, and was not destroyed. I myself believe, that, while every thing has received great improvement, and the present bears no resemblance to the past, nothing has been so changed and improved as the practice of war. For anciently, as I am informed, the Lacedaemonians and all Grecian people would for four or five months, during the season [Footnote: The campaigning season, during the summer and fine time of the year. The Peloponnesians generally invaded Attica when the corn was ripe, burning and plundering all in their route. Thucydides in his history divides the year into two parts, summer and winter.] only, invade and ravage the land of their enemies with heavy-armed and national troops, and return home again: and their ideas were so old-fashioned, or rather national, they never purchased [Footnote: Compare the old lines of Ennius:

> Non cauponantes bellum sed belligerantes
> Ferro, non auro, vitam cernamus utrique.]

an advantage from any; theirs was a legitimate and open warfare. But now you doubtless perceive, that the majority of disasters have been effected by treason; nothing is done in fair field or combat. You hear of Philip marching where he pleases, not because he commands troops of the line, but because he has attached to him a host of skirmishers, cavalry, archers, mercenaries, and the like. When with these he falls upon a people in civil dissension, and none (for mistrust) will march out to defend the country, he applies engines and besieges them. I need not mention, that he makes no difference between winter and summer, that he has no stated season of repose. You, knowing these things, reflecting on them, must not let the war approach your territories, nor get your necks broken, relying on the simplicity of the old war with the Lacedaemonians, but take the longest time beforehand for defensive measures and preparations, see that he stirs not from home, avoid any decisive engagement. For a war, if we choose, men of Athens, to pursue a right course, we have many natural advantages; such as the position of his kingdom, which we may extensively plunder and ravage, and a thousand more; but for a battle he is better trained than we are. [Footnote: Chaeronea proved the wisdom of this advice. Similar counsel was given by Pericles in the Peloponnesian war. Had the Athenians attempted to meet the invading army in the field, they must inevitably have been defeated in the early period of the war.]

Nor is it enough to adopt these resolutions and oppose him by warlike measures: you must on calculation and on principle abhor his advocates here, remembering that it is impossible to overcome your enemies abroad, until you have chastised those who are his ministers within the city. Which, by Jupiter and all the gods, you can not and will not do! You have arrived at such a pitch of folly or madness or—I know not what to call it: I am tempted often to think, that some evil genius is driving you to ruin—for the sake of scandal or envy or jest or any other cause, you command hirelings to speak, (some of whom would not deny themselves to be hirelings,) and laugh when they abuse people. And this, bad as it is, is not the worst: you have allowed these persons more liberty for their political conduct than your faithful counselors: and see what evils are caused by listening to such men with indulgence. I will mention facts that you will all remember.

In Olynthus some of the statesmen were in Philip's interest, doing every thing for him; some were on the honest side, aiming to preserve their fellow-citizens from slavery. Which party now destroyed their country? or which betrayed the cavalry, [Footnote: After Olynthus was besieged by Philip, various sallies were made from the city, some of which were successful. But the treachery of Lasthenes and his accomplices ruined all. A body of five hundred horse were led by him into an ambuscade, and captured by the besiegers. See Appendix I.] by whose betrayal Olynthus fell? The creatures of Philip; they that, while the city stood, slandered and calumniated the honest counselors so effectually, that the Olynthian people were induced to banish Apollonides.

Nor is it there only, and nowhere else, that such practice has been ruinous. In Eretria, when, after riddance of Plutarch [Footnote: When he was expelled by Phocion after the battle of Tamynae, B. C. 354.] and his mercenaries, the people got possession of their city and of Porthmus, some were for bringing the government over to you, others to Philip. His partisans were generally, rather exclusively, attended to by the wretched and unfortunate Eretrians, who at length were persuaded to expel their faithful advisers. Philip, their ally and friend, sent Hipponicus and a thousand mercenaries, demolished the walls of Porthmus, and established three rulers, Hipparchus, Automedon, Clitarchus. Since that he has driven them out of the country, twice attempting their deliverance: once he sent the troops with Eurylochus, afterward those of Parmenio.

What need of many words? In Oreus Philip's agents were Philistides, Menippus, Socrates, Thoas, and Agapaeus, who now hold the government: that was quite notorious: one Euphraeus, a man that formerly dwelt here among you, was laboring for freedom and independence. How this man was in other respects insulted and trampled on by the people of Oreus, were long to tell: but a year before the capture, discovering what Philistides and his accomplices were about, he laid an information against them for treason. A multitude then combining, having Philip for their paymaster, and acting under his direction, take Euphraeus off to prison as a disturber of the public peace. Seeing which, the people of Oreus, instead of assisting the one and beating the others to death, with them were not angry, but said his punishment was just, and rejoiced at it. So the conspirators, having full liberty of action, laid their schemes and took their measures for the surrender of the city; if any of the people observed it, they were silent and intimidated, remembering the treatment of Euphraeus; and so wretched was their condition, that on the approach of such a calamity none dared to utter a word, until the enemy drew up before the walls: then some were for defense, others for betrayal. Since the city was thus basely and wickedly taken, the traitors have held despotic rule; people who formerly rescued them, and were ready for any maltreatment of Euphraeus, they have either banished or put to death; Euphraeus killed himself, proving by deed, that he had resisted Philip honestly and purely for the good of his countrymen.

What can be the reason—perhaps you wonder—why the Olynthians and Eretrians and Orites were more indulgent to Philip's advocates than to their own? The same which operates with you. They who advise for the best can not always gratify their audience, though they would; for the safety of the state must be attended to: their opponents by the very counsel which is agreeable advance Philip's interest. One party required contribution; the other said there was no necessity: one were for war and mistrust; the other for peace, until they were ensnared. And so on for every thing else; (not to dwell on particulars;) the one made speeches to please for the moment, and gave no annoyance; the other offered salutary counsel, that was offensive. Many rights did the people surrender at last, not from any such motive of indulgence or ignorance, but submitting in the belief that all was lost, Which, by Jupiter and Apollo, I fear will be your case, when on calculation you see that nothing can be done. I pray, men of Athens, it may never come to this! Better die a thousand deaths than render homage to Philip, or sacrifice any of your faithful counselors. A fine recompense have the people of Oreus got, for trusting themselves to Philip's friends and spurning Euphraeus! Finely are the Eretrian commons rewarded, for having driven away your embassadors and yielded to Clitarchus! Yes; they are slaves, exposed to the lash and the torture. Finally he spared the Olynthians, who appointed Lasthenes to command their horse, and expelled Apollonides! It is folly and cowardice to cherish such hopes, and, while you take evil counsel and shirk every duty, and even listen to those who plead for your enemies, to think you inhabit a city of such magnitude, that you can not suffer any serious misfortune. Yea, and it is disgraceful to exclaim on any occasion, when it is too late, "Who would have expected it? However—this or that should have been done, the other left undone." Many things could the Olynthians mention now, which, if foreseen at the time would have prevented their destruction. Many could the Orites mention, many the Phocians, and each of the ruined states. But what would it avail them? As long as the vessel is safe, whether it be great or small, the mariner, the pilot, every man in turn should exert himself, and prevent its being overturned either by accident or design: but when the sea hath rolled over it, their efforts are vain. And we, likewise, O Athenians, while we are safe, with a magnificent city, plentiful resources, lofty reputation—what [Footnote: Smead remarks here on the adroitness of the orator, who, instead of applying the simile of the ship to the administration of the state, which he felt that his quick-minded hearers had already done, suddenly interrupts himself with a question, which would naturally occur to the audience.] must we do? Many of you, [Footnote: You, [Greek: oi kathaemenoi]. See my observations in the preface. I can not forbear noticing the manner in which Francis translates the following [Greek: nae Di ero]. "Let Jupiter be witness, with what integrity I shall declare my opinion." The original means nothing of the kind. It is rare that [Greek: nae Dia] can be translated literally with effect. Jacobs here has wohlan.] I dare say, have been longing to ask. Well then, I will tell you; I will move a resolution: pass it, if you please.

First, let us prepare for our own defense; provide ourselves, I mean, with ships, money, and troops—for surely, though all other people consented to be slaves, we at least ought to struggle for freedom. When we have completed our own preparations and made them apparent to the Greeks, then let us invite the rest, and send our embassadors every where with the intelligence, to Peloponnesus, to Rhodes, to Chios, to the king, I say; (for it concerns his interests, not to let Philip make universal conquest;) that, if you prevail, you may have partners of your dangers and expenses, in case of necessity, or at all events that you may delay the operations. For, since the war is against an individual, [Footnote: Because a state is a permanent power; a single man is liable to a variety of accidents, and his power terminates with his life.] not against the collected power of a state, even this may be useful; as were the embassies last year to Peloponnesus, and the remonstrances with which I and Polyeuctus, that excellent man, and Hegesippus, and Clitomachus, and Lycurgus, and the other envoys went round, and arrested Philip's progress, so that he neither attacked Ambracia nor started for Peloponnesus. I say not, however, that you should invite the rest without adopting measures to protect yourselves: it would be folly, while you sacrifice your own interest, to profess a regard for that of strangers, or to alarm others about the future, while for the present you are unconcerned. I advise not this: I bid you send supplies to the troops in Chersonesus, and do what else they require; prepare yourselves and make every effort first, then summon, gather, instruct the rest of the Greeks. That is the duty of a state possessing a dignity such as yours. If you imagine that Chalcidians or Megarians will save Greece, while you run away from the contest, you imagine wrong. Well for any of those people, if they are safe themselves. This work belongs to you: this privilege your ancestors bequeathed to you, the prize of many perilous exertions. But if every one will sit seeking his pleasure, and studying to be idle himself, never will he find others to do his work, and more than this, I fear we shall be under the necessity of doing all that we like not at one time. Were proxies to be had, our inactivity would have found them long ago; but they are not.

Such are the measures which I advise, which I propose: adopt them, and even yet, I believe, our prosperity may be re-established. If any man has better advice to offer, let him communicate it openly. Whatever you determine, I pray to all the gods for a happy result.

THE FOURTH PHILIPPIC.

THE ARGUMENT.

The subject of this Oration is the same as the last, viz., the necessity of resistance to Philip. The time of its delivery would appear to have been a little later, while Philip was yet in Thrace, and before he commenced the siege of the Propontine towns. No new event is alluded to, except the seizure of Hermias by the satrap Mentor, the exact date of which is uncertain. The orator urges here, still more strongly than he had done in the third Philippic, the necessity of applying to Persia for assistance. His advice was followed, and a negotiation was opened with that monarchy, which led to the effective relief of Perinthus. There is a remarkable passage in this speech, on the importance of general unanimity, which seems to imply that disputes had arisen between the richer and poorer classes, chiefly in regard to the application of the public revenue. The view which is here taken on the subject of the Theoric distributions is so different from the argument in the Olynthiacs, that modern critics have generally considered this Oration to be spurious. Another ground for such opinion is, that it contains various passages borrowed from other speeches, and not very skillfully put together. Yet the genuineness seems not to have been doubted by any of the ancient grammarians.

Believing, men of Athens, that the subject of your consultation is serious and momentous to the state, I will endeavor to advise what I think important. Many have been the faults, accumulated for some time past, which have brought us to this wretched condition; but none is under the circumstances so distressing as this, men of Athens; that your minds are alienated from public business; you are attentive just while you sit listening to some news, afterward you all go away, and, so far from caring for what you heard, you forget it altogether.

Well; of the extent of Philip's arrogance and ambition, as evinced in his dealings with every people, you have been informed. That it is not possible to restrain him in such course by speeches and harangues, no man can be ignorant: or, if other reasons fail to convince you, reflect on this. Whenever we have had to discuss our claims, on no occasion have we been worsted or judged in the wrong; we have still beaten and got the better of all in argument. But do his affairs go badly on this account, or ours well? By no means. For as Philip immediately proceeds, with arms in his hand, to put all he possesses boldly at stake, while we with our equities, the speakers as well as the hearers, are sitting still, actions (naturally enough) outstrip words, and people attend not to what we have argued or may argue, but to what we do, All our doings are not likely to protect any of our injured neighbors: I need not say more upon the subject. Therefore, as the states are divided into two parties, one that would neither hold arbitrary government nor submit to it, but live under free and equal laws; another desiring to govern their fellow-citizens, and be subject to some third power, by whose assistance they hope to accomplish that object; the partisans of Philip, [Footnote: I agree with Pabst and Auger that [Greek: ekeinon] signifies Philip. Schaefer takes it neutrally.] who desire tyranny and despotism, have every where prevailed, and I know not whether there is any state left, besides our own, with a popular constitution firmly established. And those, that hold the government through him, have prevailed by all the means efficacious in worldly affairs; principally and mainly, by having a person to bribe the corruptible; secondly, a point no less important, by having at their command, at whatever season they required, an army to put down their opponents. We, men of Athens, are not only in these respects behindhand; we can not even be awaked; like men that have drunk mandrake [Footnote: Used for a powerful opiate by the ancients. It is called Mandragora also in English. See Othello, Act III. Sc. 3.

    Not poppy, nor mandragora,
  Nor all the drowsy sirups of the world,
  Shall ever medicine thee to that sweet sleep
  Which thou ow'dst yesterday.]

or some other sleeping potion; and methinks—for I judge the truth must be spoken—we are by reason thereof held in such disrepute and contempt, that, among the states in imminent danger, some dispute with us for the lead, some for the place of congress; others have resolved to defend themselves separately rather than in union with us.

Why am I so particular in mentioning these things? I seek not to give offense; so help me all the powers of heaven! I wish, men of Athens, to make it clear and manifest to you all, that habitual sloth and indolence, the same in public matters as in private life, is not immediately felt on every occasion of neglect, but shows itself in the general result. [Footnote: Auger: "presentent a la fin un total effrayant."] Look at Serrium and Doriscus; which were first disregarded after the peace. Their names perhaps are unknown to many of you: yet your careless abandonment of these lost Thrace and Cersobleptes your ally. Again, seeing these places neglected and unsupported by you, he demolished Porthmus, and raised a tyrant in Euboea like a fortress against Attica. This being disregarded, Megara was very nearly taken. You were insensible, indifferent to all his aggressions; gave no intimation that you would not permit their continuance. He purchased Antrones, [Footnote: A town in Thessaly. We do not know all the details of Philip's proceedings in that country, but we have seen enough to know, first under the guise of a protector he was not far short of being the master of the Thessalian people. Some of these towns were actually in his possession, as Pherae and Pagasae. But that the Thesssalians were never entirely subjugated to Macedonia, and still retained a hankering after independence, was proved at a later period by their desertion of Antipater.] and not long after had got Oreus into his power. Many transactions I omit; Pherae, the march against Ambracia, the massacres at Elis, [Footnote: The Elean exiles, having engaged in their service a body of the Phocian mercenaries, made an incursion into Elis, but were repelled. A large number of prisoners were taken and put to death. This happened B. C. 343. The government of Elis was at that time in the hands of a Macedonian party.] and numberless others: for I have not entered upon these details, to enumerate the people whom Philip has oppressed and wronged, but to show you that Philip will not desist from wronging all people and pursuing his conquests, until an effort is made to prevent him.

There are persons whose custom it is, before they hear any speech in the debate, to ask immediately—"What must we do?"—not with the intention of doing what they are told (or they would be the most serviceable of men), but in order to get rid of the speaker. Nevertheless, you should be advised what to do. First, O my countrymen, you must be firmly convinced in your minds, that Philip is at war with our state, and has broken the peace; that, while he is inimical and hostile to the whole of Athens, to the ground of Athens, and I may add, to the gods in Athens, (may they exterminate him!) there is nothing which he strives and plots against so much as our constitution, nothing in the world that he is so anxious about, as its destruction. And thereunto he is driven in some sort by necessity. Consider. He wishes for empire: he believes you to be his only opponents. He has been a long time injuring you, as his own conscience best informs him; for by means of your possessions, which he is able to enjoy, he secures all the rest of his kingdom: had he given up Amphipolis and Potidaea, he would not have deemed himself safe even in Macedonia. He knows therefore, both that he is plotting against you, and that you are aware of it; and, supposing you to have common sense, he judges that you detest him as you ought. Besides these important considerations, he is assured that, though he became master of every thing else, nothing can be safe for him while you are under popular government: should any reverse ever befall him, (and many may happen to a man,) all who are now under constraint will come for refuge to you. For you are not inclined yourselves to encroach and usurp dominion; but famous rather for checking the usurper or depriving him of his conquests, ever ready to molest the aspirants for empire, and vindicate the liberty of all nations. He would not like that a free spirit should proceed from Athens, to watch the occasions of his weakness; nor is such reasoning foolish or idle. First then you must assume, that he is an irreconcilable enemy of our constitution and democracy; secondly, you must be convinced, that all his operations and contrivances are designed for the injury of our state. None of you can be so silly as to suppose, that Philip covets those miseries in Thrace, (for what else can one call Drongilus and Cabyle and Mastira and the places which he is said now to occupy?) and that to get possession of them he endures hardships and winters and the utmost peril, but covets not the harbors of Athens, the docks, the galleys, the silver mines, the revenues of such value, the place and the glory—never may he or any other man obtain these by the conquest of our city!—or that he will suffer you to keep these things, while for the sake of the barley and millet in Thracian caverns he winters in the midst of horrors. [Footnote: See the note in the Oration on the Chersonese, page 108, where the same words nearly are repeated.] Impossible. The object of that and every other enterprise of Philip is, to become master here.

So should every man be persuaded and convinced; and therefore, I say, should not call upon your faithful and upright counselor to move a resolution for war: [Footnote: He deprecates here, as elsewhere, the factious proceedings of certain opponents, who sought to fasten the responsibility of a war on the orator, by forcing him to propose a decree.

This (argues Demosthenes) was unnecessary, as they were at war already.] such were the part of men seeking an enemy to fight with, not men forwarding the interests of the state. Only see. Suppose for the first breach of the treaty by Philip, or for the second or third, (for there is a series of breaches,) any one had made a motion for war with him, and Philip, just as he has now without such motion, had aided the Cardians, would not the mover have been sacrificed? [Footnote: Pabst, following Wolf, takes this in the more limited sense of being carried off to prison: ins Gefängniss geworfen. The English translators, who have "torn to pieces," understand the word in the same sense that I do, as meaning generally "destroyed, exterminated."] would not all have imputed Philip's aid of the Cardians to that cause? Don't then look for a person to vent your anger on for Philip's trespasses, to throw to Philip's hirelings to be torn in pieces. Do not, after yourselves voting for war, dispute with each other, whether you ought or ought not to have done so. As Philip conducts the war, so resist him: furnish those who are resisting him now [Footnote: Referring to Diopithes and his troops in the Chersonese.] with money and what else they demand; pay your contributions, men of Athens, provide an army, swift-sailing galleys, horses, transports, all the materials of war. Our present mode of operation is ridiculous; and by the gods I believe, that Philip could not wish our republic to take any other course than what ye now pursue. You miss your time, waste your money, look for a person to manage your affairs, are discontented, accuse one another. How all this comes about, I will explain, and how it may cease I will inform you.

Nothing, O men of Athens, have you ever set on foot or contrived rightly in the beginning: you always follow the event, stop when you are too late, on any new occurrence prepare and bustle again. But that is not the way of proceeding. It is never possible with sudden levies to perform any essential service. You must establish an army, provide maintenance for it, and paymasters, and commissaries, so ordering it that the strictest care be taken of your funds; demand from those officers an account of the expenditure, from your general an account of the campaign; and leave not the general any excuse for sailing elsewhere or prosecuting another enterprise. If ye so act and so resolve in earnest, you will compel Philip to observe a just peace and remain in his own country, or will contend with him on equal terms; and perhaps, Athenians, perhaps, as you now inquire what Philip is doing, and whither marching, so he may be anxious to learn, whither the troops of Athens are bound, and where they will make their appearance.

Should any man think that these are affairs of great expense and toil and difficulty, he thinks rightly enough: but let him consider what the consequences to Athens must be, if she refuse so to act, and he will find it is our interest to perform our duties cheerfully. Suppose you had some god for your surety—for certainly no mortal could guarantee a thing so fortunate—that, although you kept quiet and sacrificed every thing, Philip would not attack you at last, yet, by Jupiter and all the gods, it would be disgraceful, unworthy of yourselves, of the dignity of your state, and the deeds of your ancestors, for the sake of selfish indolence to abandon the rest of Greece to servitude. For my part, I would rather die than have advised such a course: however, if any other man advises it, and can prevail on you, be it so; make no defense, abandon all. But if no man holds such an opinion, if on the contrary we all foresee, that, the more we permit Philip to conquer, the more fierce and formidable an enemy we shall find him, what subterfuge remains? what excuse for delay? Or when, O Athenians, shall we be willing to act as becomes us? Peradventure, when there is some necessity. But what may be called the necessity of freemen is not only come, but past long ago; and that of slaves you must surely deprecate. What is the difference? To a freeman shame for what is occurring is the strongest necessity; I know of none stronger that can be mentioned: to a slave, stripes and bodily chastisement; abominable things! too shocking to name!

To be backward, men of Athens, in performing those services to which the person and property of every one are liable, is wrong, very wrong, and yet it admits of some excuse: but refusing even to bear what is necessary to be heard, and fit to be considered, this calls for the severest censure. Your practice however is, neither to attend until the business actually presses, as it does now, nor to deliberate about any thing at leisure. When Philip is preparing, you, instead of doing the like and making counter-preparation, remain listless, and, if any one speaks a word, clamor him down: when you receive news that any place is lost or besieged, then you listen and prepare. But the time to have heard and consulted was then when you declined; the time to act and employ your preparations is now that you are hearing. Such being your habits, you are the only people who adopt this singular course: others deliberate usually before action, you deliberate after action. One thing [Footnote: He means negotiation with Persia, to obtain pecuniary assistance.] remains, which should have been done long ago, but even yet is not too late: I will mention it. Nothing in the world does Athens need so much, as money for approaching exigencies. Lucky events have occurred, and, if we rightly improve them, perhaps good service may be done. In the first place, those, [Footnote: The Thracians, who had always been regarded as benefactors of the Persian king, since they assisted Darius on his invasion of Scythia. Philip was making war in Thrace at this time, and had subjected a considerable part of the country.] whom the king trusts and regards as his benefactors, are at enmity and war with Philip. Secondly, the agent and confidant [Footnote: Hermias, governor of Atarneus in Mysia, who for his treasonable practices against Artaxerxes was seized by Mentor and sent in chains to Susa, where he was put to death. He was a friend of Aristotle, who was at his court, when he was taken prisoner. The philosopher afterward married his sister.] of all Philip's preparations against the king has been snatched off, and the king will hear all the proceedings, not from Athenian accusers, whom he might consider to be speaking for their own interests, but from the acting minister himself; the charges therefore will be credible, and the only remaining argument for our embassadors will be, one which the Persian monarch will rejoice to hear, that we should take common vengeance on the injurer of both, and that Philip is much more formidable to the king, if he attack us first; for, should we be left in the lurch and suffer any mishap, he will march against the king without fear. On all these matters then I advise that you dispatch an embassy to confer with the king, and put aside that nonsense which has so often damaged you—"the barbarian," forsooth, "the common enemy"—and the like. I confess, when I see a man alarmed at a prince in Susa and Ecbatana, and declaring him to be an enemy of Athens, him that formerly [Footnote: In the confederate war, when the Persian fleet enabled Conon to defeat the Lacedaemonians at Onidus, B. C. 394.] assisted in re-establishing her power, and lately made overtures [Footnote: Artaxerxes had applied both to Athens and Lacedaemon to aid him in the recovery of Egypt, which for many years had been held in a state of revolt. Both these states refused to assist him. He then applied to Thebes and Argos, each of which sent an auxiliary force.]—if you did not accept them, but voted refusal, the fault is not his—while the same man speaks a different language of one who is close at our doors, and growing up in the centre of Greece to be the plunderer of her people; I marvel, I dread this man, whoever he is, because he dreads not Philip.

There is another thing too, the attacking of which by unjust reproach and improper language hurts the state, and affords an excuse to men who are unwilling to perform any public duty: indeed you will find that every failure to discharge the obligation of a citizen is attributable to this. I am really afraid to discuss the matter; however, I will speak out.

I believe I can suggest, for the advantage of the state, a plea for the poor against the rich, and for men of property against the indigent; could we remove the clamor which some persons unfairly raise about the theatric fund, [Footnote: Boeckh, Schaefer, and others, regard it as conclusive against the genuineness of this Oration, that a different view is here taken on the subject of the Theoric fund from that which Demosthenes had expressed in the Olynthiacs. And certainly it is a strong argument. It is possible, however, that circumstances may have induced him to modify his opinion, or he may have thought it dangerous to meddle with the law of Eubulus at the present crisis, which called for the greatest unanimity among all classes. We may partly gather from this speech, that there had been some agitation among the lower classes, occasioned by the complaints of the wealthy against this law. Any agitation tending to a spirit of communism must have been extremely dangerous at Athens, where the people had such power of muleting the higher classes by their votes in the popular assembly and courts of justice. It might therefore be better to let the people alone with their theatrical treats, their fees and largesses, than to provoke retaliation by abridging such enjoyments. Leland observes on the subject as follows—"All that the orator here says in defense of the theatrical appointments is expressed with a caution and reserve quite opposite to his usual openness and freedom; and which plainly betray a consciousness of his being inconsistent with his former sentiments. How far he may be excused by the supposed necessity of yielding to the violent prepossessions of the people, and giving up a favorite point, I can not pretend to determine. But it is certainly not very honorable to Demosthenes, to suppose with Ulpian, that his former opposition was merely personal, and that the death of Eubulus now put an end to it."] and the fear that it can not stand without some signal mischief. No greater help to our affairs could we introduce; [Footnote: Viz., than the removal of this clamor and alarm about the theatric fund.] none that would more strengthen the whole community. Look at it thus. I will commence on behalf of those who are considered the needy class. There was a time with us, not long ago, when only a hundred and thirty talents came into the state; [Footnote: This must be understood (according to Boeckh) of the tribute only, which came in from the allies. The total revenue of Athens must have greatly exceeded this.] and among the persons qualified to command ships or pay property-tax, there was not one who claimed exemption from his duty because no surplus existed: [Footnote: There was as much ground for legal exemption then as there is now; and yet it was never claimed. Why should the rich seek to be relieved from their burdens because of an abundance of revenue? That abundance is for the general benefit of the state, not for theirs in particular. Such appears to be the argument, perhaps not quite satisfactory; but such it is. Pabst, apparently reading [Greek: aph heautou], has: der nicht aus eigenem Antrieb seine Schuldigkeit zu thun bereit war, weil kein Gelduberschuss vorhanden war.] galleys sailed, money was forthcoming, every thing needful was done. Since that time fortune happily has increased the revenue, and four hundred talents come in instead of one, without loss to any men of property, but with gain to them; for all the wealthy come for their share of the fund, and they are welcome to it. [Footnote: I. e. the Theoric fund, in which every member of the commonwealth had a right to share.] Why then do we reproach one another on this account, and make it an excuse for declining our duties, unless we grudge the relief given by fortune to the poor? I would be sorry to blame them myself, and I think it not right. In private families I never see a young man behaving so to his elders, so unfeeling or so unreasonable, as to refuse to do any thing himself, unless all the rest will do what he does. Such a person would certainly be amenable to the laws against undutiful conduct: [Footnote: Pabst: die Gesetze wegen ungebuhrlicher Behandlung der Eltern. [Greek: Kakosis], "maltreatment", was a technical term in the Attic law, denoting a failure of duty on the part of husbands, children, or guardians, toward their wives, parents, or wards, for which they were liable to be tried and punished in a suit called [Greek: kakoseos dikae]. The jurisdiction over this offense belonged to the Archon, who was the protector of all family rights.] for I ween there is a tribute assigned to parents both by nature and by law, which ought to be cheerfully offered and amply paid. Accordingly, as each individual among us hath a parent, so should we regard the whole people as parents of the state, and, so far from depriving them of what the state bestows, we ought, in the absence of such bounty, to find other means to keep them from destitution. If the rich will adopt this principle, I think they will act both justly and wisely; for to deprive any class of a necessary provision, is to unite them in disaffection to the commonwealth.

To the poor I would recommend, that they remove the cause, which makes men of property discontented with the present system, and excites their just complaints. I shall take the same course on behalf of the wealthy as I did just now, and not hesitate to speak the truth. There can not, I believe, be found a wretch so hard-hearted—I will not say among Athenians, but among any other people—who would be sorry to see poor men, men without the necessaries of life, receiving these bounties. Where then is the pinch [Footnote: The expression "Where is the rub?" would be still nearer to the original, and the expression reminds one of the line in Hamlet:

To sleep! perchance to dream! ay, there's the rub.

Reiske says the simile is taken from the collision of chariots in the race; but this is confining it too much. His vernacular explanation is: woran stosst es sich? wo ist der Haken? Pabst has: woran stosst sich die Sache, und was erzeugt den Verdruss?] of the matter? where the difficulty? When they see certain persons transferring the usage established for the public revenue to private property, and the orator becoming immediately powerful with you, yea, (so far as privilege can make him,) immortal, and your secret vote contradicting your public clamor. [Footnote: Having admonished the higher classes to pay their property-tax and perform their public services cheerfully, and without seeking to be relieved at the expense of the public revenue, he proceeds to remind the lower classes of their duty. He warns them, that, while they receive a benefit from the funds of the state, they must not endeavor to increase those funds unduly by an invasion of the rights of property. His language is not open, but would easily be understood by his audience. The Athenians ought not to promote lawsuits to increase court-fees; not to encourage prosecutions against wealthy citizens, in order to obtain fines and confiscations. He insinuates that there was too much cause for complaint already. [Greek: Ton legonta] is, not as Schaefer contends, the rich man pleading his cause before the people, but, as Wolf explains it, the popular orator or informer, who speedily rose to favor and influence, of which it was not easy to deprive him. His opponent, speaking in a just cause, might be applauded at the time, but the votes showed what was the real bias of the people. In courts of justice at Athens the voting was usually by a secret ballot; (see my article Psephus in the Archaeological Dictionary;) and there being a large number of jurors, it would be difficult to discover by whose votes the verdict was obtained. It is impossible to read the frequent appeals made by Athenian speakers to the passions and prejudices of the jury, without seeing that there was some ground for the insinuations of the orator in this passage.] Hence arises mistrust, hence indignation. We ought, O ye men of Athens, to have a just communion of political rights; the opulent holding themselves secure in their fortunes, and without fear of losing them, yet in time of danger imparting their substance freely for the defense of their country; while the rest consider the public revenue as public, and receive their share, but look on private property as belonging to the individual owner. Thus it is that a small commonwealth becomes great, and a great one is preserved. To speak generally then, such are the obligations of each class; to insure their performance according to law, some regulation should be made.

The causes of our present troubles and embarrassment are many and of ancient date: if you are willing to hear, I will declare them. You have quitted, O Athenians, the position in which your ancestors left you; you have been persuaded by these politicians, that to stand foremost of the Greeks, to keep a permanent force and redress injured nations, is all vanity and idle expense; you imagine that to live in quiet, to perform no duty, to abandon one thing after another and let strangers seize on all, brings with it marvelous welfare and abundant security. By such means a stranger has advanced to the post which you ought to have occupied, has become prosperous and great, and made large conquest; naturally enough. A prize there was, noble, great, and glorious, one for which the mightiest states were contending all along; but as the Lacedaemonians were humbled, the Thebans had their hands full through the Phocian war, and we took no regard, he carried it off without competition. The result has been, to others terror, to him a vast alliance and extended power; while difficulties so many and so distressing surround the Greeks, that even advice is not easy to be found.

Yet, perilous as I conceive the present crisis to be for all, no people are in such danger as you, men of Athens; not only because Philip's designs are especially aimed at you, but because of all people you are the most remiss. If, seeing the abundance of commodities and cheapness in your market, you are beguiled into a belief that the state is in no danger, your judgment is neither becoming nor correct. A market or a fair one may, from such appearances, judge to be well or ill supplied: but for a state, which every aspirant for the empire of Greece has deemed to be alone capable of opposing him, and defending the liberty of all—for such a state! verily her marketable commodities are not the test of prosperity, but this—whether she can depend on the good-will of her allies; whether she is puissant in arms. On behalf of such a state these are the things to be considered; and in these respects your condition is wretched and deplorable. You will understand it by a simple reflection. When have the affairs of Greece been in the greatest confusion? No other time could any man point out but the present. In former times Greece was divided into two parties, that of the Lacedaemonians and ours: some of the Greeks were subject to us, some to them. The Persian, on his own account, was mistrusted equally by all, but he used to make friends of the vanquished parties, and retain their confidence, until he put them on an equality with the other side; after which those that he succored would hate him as much as his original enemies. Now however the king is on friendly terms with all the Greeks, though least friendly with us, unless we put matters right. Now too there are protectors [Footnote: This is said with some irony: many states offer to come forward as protectors, but only on condition of taking the lead: they will not join the common cause on fair terms. Many of the translations miss the sense here. Leland understands it rightly: "there are several cities which affect the character of guardians and protectors." Auger confounds this sentence with the next: "il s' eleve de tous cotes plusieurs puissances qui aspirent toutes a la primaute."] springing up in every quarter, and all claim the precedency, though some indeed have abandoned the cause, or envy and distrust each other—more shame for them—and every state is isolated, Argives, Thebans, Lacedaemonians, Corinthians, Arcadians, and ourselves. But, divided as Greece is among so many parties and so many leaderships, if I must speak the truth freely, there is no state whose offices and halls of council appear more deserted by Grecian politics than ours. And no wonder; when neither friendship, nor confidence, nor fear leads any to negotiate with us.

This, ye men of Athens, has come not from any single cause, (or you might easily mend it,) but from a great variety and long series of errors. I will not stop to recount them, but will mention one, to which all may be referred, beseeching you not to be offended, if I boldly speak the truth.

Your interests are sold on every favorable opportunity: you partake of the idleness and ease, under the charm whereof you resent not your wrongs; while other persons get the reward. [Footnote: Schaefer rightly explains [Greek: timas] to mean the price received for treason. But most of the translators, following Wolf, understand it to mean the honors won by Philip. [Greek: Tois adikousin] is rendered by Auger, Leland, and Francis, "the traitors." I think it rather refers to, or at least includes, the enemies who profited by the treason, and made conquests from Athens: of course meaning Philip in particular.] Into all these cases I could not enter now: but when any question about Philip arises, some one starts up directly and says—"We must have no trifling, no proposal of war"—and then goes on to say—"What a blessing it is to be at peace! what a grievance to maintain a large army!"—and again—"Certain persons wish to plunder the treasury"—and other arguments they urge, no doubt, in the full conviction of their truth. [Footnote: There is no difficulty in this, if we understand it to be ironical; and no need of any amendment.] But surely there is no need of persuading you to observe peace, you that sit here persuaded already. It is Philip (who is making war) that needs persuasion: prevail on him, and all is ready on your part. We should consider as grievous, not what we expend for our deliverance, but what we shall suffer in case of refusal. Plunder of the treasury should be prevented by devising a plan for its safe custody, not by abandoning our interests. Yet this very thing makes me indignant, that some of you are pained at the thought of your treasury being robbed, though it depends on yourselves to guard it and to punish the criminal, but are not pained to see Philip plundering Greece, plundering as he does one people after another, to forward his designs upon you.

How comes it, ye men of Athens, that of this flagrant aggressor, this capturer of cities, no one has ever declared that he commits hostility or injustice, while those who counsel against submission and sacrifice are charged as the authors of war? The reason is, that people wish to cast upon your faithful counselors the blame of any untoward events in the war; for war must necessarily be attended with many misfortunes. They believe that, if you resist Philip with one heart and mind, you will prevail against him, and they can be hirelings no longer; but that if on the first outcry [Footnote: Leland: "the first unhappy accident." Francis gives the right meaning, but with too many words; "the first tumults occasioned by any unfortunate success." Spillau: "the first alarm."] you arraign certain persons and bring them to trial, they by accusing such persons will gain a double advantage, repute among the Athenians and recompense from Philip; and that you will punish your friendly advisers for a cause for which you ought to punish the traitors. Such are the hopes, such the contrivance of these charges, "that certain persons wish to kindle a war." I am sure, however, that, without any Athenian moving a declaration of war, Philip has taken many of our possessions, and has recently sent succor to Cardia. If we choose to assume that he is not making war against us, he would be the simplest of mankind to convince us of our mistake: for when the sufferers disclaim the injury, what should the offenders do? But when he marches to attack us, what shall we say then? He will assure us that he is not making war, as he assured the Orites, when his troops were in their country, as he assured the Pheraeans before he assaulted their walls, and the Olynthians in the first instance, until he was in their territories with his army. Shall we then say, that persons who bid us defend ourselves kindle a war? If so, we must be slaves; for nothing else remains.

But remember: you have more at stake than some other people. Philip desires not to subjugate your city, but to destroy it utterly. He is convinced, you will not submit to be slaves; if you were inclined, you would not know how, having been accustomed to command: you will be able, should occasion offer, to give him more trouble than any people in the world. For this reason he will show us no mercy, if he get us into his power: and therefore you must make up your minds, that the struggle will be one for life and death. These persons, who have openly sold themselves to Philip, you must execrate, you must beat their brains out: for it is impossible, I say impossible, to vanquish your foreign enemies, until you have punished your enemies within the city: these are the stumbling-blocks that must cripple your efforts against the foreigner.

From what cause, do ye think, Philip insults you now; (for his conduct, in my judgment, amounts to nothing less;) and while he deceives other people by doing them services—this at least is something—you he threatens already? For example, the Thessalians by many benefits he seduced into their present servitude: no man can tell how he cheated the poor Olynthians, giving them first Potidaea and many other places: now he is luring the Thebans, having delivered up Boeotia to them, and freed them from a tedious and harassing war. Of these people, who each got a certain advantage, some have suffered what is notorious to all, others have yet to suffer what may befall them. As to yourselves; the amount of your losses I do not mention: but in the very making of the peace how have you been deceived! how plundered! Lost you not the Phocians, Thermopylae, country toward Thrace, Doriscus, Serrium, Cersobleptes himself? Holds he not Cardia now, and avows it? Why then does he behave thus to other people, and in a different way to you? Because our city is the only one where liberty is allowed to speak for the enemy, where a man taking a bribe may safely address the people, though they have been deprived of their possessions. It was not safe at Olynthus to advocate Philip's cause, without the Olynthian people sharing the benefit by possession of Potidaea. It was not safe to advocate Philip's cause in Thessaly, without the people of Thessaly sharing the benefit, by Philip's expelling their tyrants and restoring the Pylaean Synod. It was not safe at Thebes, until he restored Boeotia to them, and destroyed the Phocians. But at Athens, though Philip has taken from you Amphipolis and the Cardian territory, and is even turning Euboea into a hostile post, and advancing to attack Byzantium, it is safe to speak on Philip's behalf. Yea, among these men, some have risen rapidly from poverty to wealth, from meanness and obscurity to repute and honor, while you, on the contrary, have fallen from honor to obscurity, from wealth to indigence. For the riches of a state I consider to be allies, confidence, good-will; of all which you are destitute. And by your neglecting these things and suffering your interests thus to be swept away, Philip has grown prosperous and mighty, formidable to all the Greeks and barbarians, while you are forlorn and abject, in the abundance of your market magnificent, but in your national defenses ridiculous. [Footnote: The whole of the foregoing passage is taken, with some little variation, from the speech on the Chersonese. It certainly would seem strange, if this Oration had been forged by any grammarian, that he should have borrowed thus by wholesale from Demosthenes. There is perhaps less difficulty in the supposition that Demosthenes repeated his own words.]

Some of our orators, I observe, take not the same thought for you as for themselves. They say that you should keep quiet, though you are injured; but they can not themselves keep quiet among you, though no one injures them. Come, raillery apart, suppose you were thus questioned, Aristodemus, [Footnote: This man was a tragic actor, and charged by Demosthenes with being a partisan of Philip. He was the first person who proposed peace with Macedonia, shortly before the embassy of ten. See the Argument to the Oration on the Peace.]—"Tell me, as you know perfectly well, what every one else knows, that the life of private men is secure and free from trouble and danger, while that of statesmen is exposed to scandal [Footnote: I have taken [Greek: philaition] in the passive sense, as it is explained by Reiske and Schaefer, though it scarcely suits the character of the word. Compare Shakspeare, Henry V. Act IV. Sc. 1.

> O hard condition, twin-born with greatness,
> Subjected to the breath of every fool!
> What infinite heart's ease must kings neglect
> That private men enjoy!]

and misfortune, full of trials and hardships every day, how comes it that you prefer, not the quiet and easy life, but the one surrounded with peril?"—what should you say? If we admitted the truth of what would be your best possible answer, namely, that all you do is for honor and renown, I wonder what puts it into your head, that you ought from such motives to exert yourself and undergo toil and danger, while you advise the state to give up exertion and remain idle. You can not surely allege, that Aristodemus ought to be of importance at Athens, and Athens to be of no account among the Greeks. Nor again do I see, that for the commonwealth it is safe to mind her own affairs only, and hazardous for you, not to be a superlative busy-body. [Footnote: All the translators have mistaken [Greek: ton allon pleon], which is simply "more than others," as Wolf explains it.] On the contrary, to you I see the utmost peril from your meddling and over-meddling, to the commonwealth peril from her inactivity. But I suppose, you inherit a reputation from your father and grandfather, which it were disgraceful in your own person to extinguish, whereas the ancestry of the state was ignoble and mean. This again is not so. Your father was a thief, [Footnote: This seems to shock Leland, who spoils the pungency of the expression, by rendering it: "Your father was like you, and therefore base and infamous." Auger remarks: "L'invective de Demosthene est fort eloquente, mais bien violente. L'amour de la patrie, contre laquelle sans doute agissait Aristodeme, peut seul en excuser la vivacite."] if he resembled you, whereas by the ancestors of the commonwealth, as all men know, the Greeks have twice been rescued from the brink of destruction. Truly the behaviour of some persons, in private and in public, is neither equitable nor constitutional. How is it equitable, that certain of these men, returned from prison, should not know themselves, while the state, that once protected all Greece and held the foremost place, is sunk in ignominy and humiliation?

Much could I add on many points, but I will forbear. It is not, I believe, to lack of words that our distresses have been owing either now or heretofore. The mischief is when you, after listening to sound arguments, and all agreeing in their justice, sit to hear with equal favor those who try to defeat and pervert them; not that you are ignorant of the men; (you are certain at the first glance, who speak for hire and are Philip's political agents, and who speak sincerely for your good;) your object is to find fault with these, turn the thing into laughter and raillery, and escape the performance of your duty.

Such is the truth, spoken with perfect freedom, purely from good-will and for the best: not a speech fraught with flattery and mischief and deceit, to earn money for the speaker, and to put the commonwealth into the hands of our enemies. I say, you must either desist from these practices, or blame none but yourselves for the wretched condition of your affairs.

Printed in Great Britain
by Amazon